MW00782038

Myth-Busters

Torrance, California

© 2009 Bristol Works, Inc.
Rose Publishing, Inc.
4733 Torrance Blvd., #259
Torrance, California 90503 U.S.A.
Email: info@rose-publishing.com
www.rose-publishing.com

Includes these Rose Publishing Titles:

Intelligent Design ©2009 Bristol Works, Inc.
        Authors: William A. Dembski, PhD; Sean McDowell, MA
10 Questions & Answers on Atheism & Agnosticism ©2007 Bristol Works, Inc.
        Authors: Norman L. Geisler, MA, ThB, PhD; Alex McFarland, MA; Robert Velarde
Pop Spirituality and the Truth ©2009 Bristol Works, Inc.
        Author: Timothy Paul Jones, EdD
10 Questions & Answers on Angels ©2008 Bristol Works, Inc.
        Principal Author: Robert M. Bowman, Jr., MA
        General Editor: Paul Carden
Jesus: Fact and Fiction ©2008 Bristol Works, Inc.
        Principal Author: Robert M. Bowman, Jr., MA
        General Editor: Paul Carden
Evidence for the Resurrection ©2004 RW Research, Inc.
Why Trust the Bible? ©2007 Bristol Works, Inc.
        Author: Timothy Paul Jones, EdD
What's So Great About Heaven ©2009 Bristol Works, Inc.
        Author: Benjamin Galan, MTS, ThM

Many of these titles are available as individual pamphlets, as wall charts, and as ready-to-use PowerPoint® presentations.

Library of Congress Cataloging-in-Publication Data

Myth-busters.
        p. cm. – (Rose Bible basics)
    ISBN 978-1-59636-345-8 (pbk.)
    1. Theology, Doctrinal–Popular works. 2. Apologetics.
    BT77.M97 2009
    230'.0462–dc22

                            2009023873

Printed in China
010609R

Myth-Busters

Contents

Continued
on next
page
→

Myth-Busters

Contents

Myths about God & Science

Myth: Darwinian evolution is a proven fact.

Myth: Evolution can explain life's origin.

Myth: Intelligent Design is not science.

Myth: There's no evidence that the universe is designed.

What Is Intelligent Design?

INTELLIGENT DESIGN

Intelligent design is the study of patterns in nature that are best explained as the result of intelligence. Intelligent design (abbreviated ID) shouldn't be controversial. Archaeologists, forensic scientists, and SETI researchers (scientists looking for signs of intelligence from outer space) are all doing intelligent design research. ID is controversial because it claims to find signs of intelligence in biology. This raises the question of who the designer could be.

© Mike Norton

OLD-STYLE DESIGN

Life looks designed. But is it actually designed? The biblical writers claim that the natural world displays knowledge of the Creator (Psalm 19:1–2; Romans 1:20–21). In the early 1800s, William Paley gave his famous Watchmaker Argument in which he reasoned that finding a watch lying in a field would indicate purposeful design rather than the outworking of purely natural forces.[1] Paley believed that living organisms bore the same design features as a watch.

DARWIN'S SHADOW

Until the publication of Charles Darwin's *Origin of Species* in 1859, most scientists and philosophers found the evidence for design in biology persuasive. Yet, according to biologist Francisco Ayala, "It was Darwin's greatest accomplishment to show that the complex organization and functionality of living beings can be explained as the result of a natural process—natural selection—without any need to resort to a Creator or other external agent."[2] Darwinism has since been the dominant viewpoint.

Yet despite its widespread acceptance, Darwinism faces a radical challenge from the theory of intelligent design (ID). In fact, the evidence for design in biology has become overwhelming.[3] Past design arguments largely failed because they lacked precise methods for design recognition. ID theorists today have developed a rigorous scientific method for detecting design, known as specified complexity.

William Paley was a Christian apologist, born in 1743 in England. His most famous work is *Natural Theology; or, Evidences of the Existence and Attributes of the Deity.* Paley argued that certain biological features in nature bore the marks of a Designer, much as the interworking parts of a watch point to a Watchmaker.

SPECIFIED COMPLEXITY

Specified complexity is the fingerprint of design. For something to exhibit specified complexity it must be hard to reproduce by chance (complex) and it must match an independently given pattern (specified). Any mountain you see is complex. It would be highly unlikely for the forces of nature to reproduce its exact shape anywhere else. But Mt. Rushmore isn't just complex. It's also specified—it matches the faces of four U.S. presidents. Because Mt. Rushmore is complex and specified, we know it's designed.

© William Davies

How Does ID Differ from Creationism and Evolution?

One of the most commonly asked questions about ID is how it differs from creationism and evolution.

EVOLUTION

"Evolution" can be defined in several ways. One definition is simply change over time. Another is that organisms adapt to their changing environments. A popular example is the variation in finch beak sizes as the result of changing weather patterns. The Galapagos Islands are home to thirteen different kinds of finches. Finch beak size is a trait that has been found to fluctuate naturally as the environment goes through seasons of drought. This is small-scale evolution, known as **microevolution**, and does nothing to explain the origin of finches.

The controversial claim is that microevolution leads inevitably to **macroevolution** (a.k.a. Darwinian evolution). Macroevolution makes two big claims:

1. All organisms trace their lineage back through time to a common ancestor. This is often called "universal common ancestry" or "common descent."

2. The mechanism that drives common ancestry is natural selection acting on random variation. This is an unguided material process that gives no evidence of purpose or design.

Darwin believed that nature (not God) would select the fittest organisms to survive in their environment and then produce offspring. The controversy is whether this process can generate entirely new species, as Darwin claimed.

Most ID theorists are skeptical of common descent, but unanimously agree in regarding Darwin's mechanism of natural selection acting on random variation as only a minor part in the history of life. ID theorists are skeptical that Darwin's mechanism is sufficient to generate all the complexity and diversity of life. Furthermore, they also agree that organisms show clear, scientific evidence of design.

Charles Darwin was born in England on February 12, 1809. While Darwin wrote many books—including *The Descent of Man, and Selection in Relation to Sex*—he is best known for *The Origin of Species*, in which he offers natural selection as the driving force of evolution.

CREATIONISM

Creationism holds that the universe was created by a Supreme Being. There are young-earth creationists (YECs) and old-earth creationists (OECs). YECs begin with a particular interpretation of Genesis specifying that:

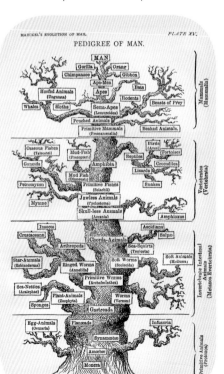

✱ God created the earth in six 24-hour days,

✱ the universe is approximately 10,000 years old,

✱ all fossils worldwide are the result of Noah's global flood.

OECs accept standard scientific dating, which places the Earth at roughly 4.5 billion years old and the universe at 13.7 billion years old. They interpret Genesis in light of these scientific facts. While OECs reject macroevolution, they accept microevolution as God's method of adapting existing species to their changing environments.

Though often confused with creationism, ID is distinct from it. Rather than assume a particular interpretation of Genesis, ID is committed to investigating the natural world through methods developed within the scientific community.[4] Given what the natural world reveals about itself, its proponents argue that intelligence best explains certain patterns in nature.

Why Is Design Important?

In *Darwin's Dangerous Idea*, atheist philosopher Daniel Dennett suggests that religious believers who talk their children out of believing Darwinian evolution should be caged in "cultural zoos" or else quarantined because they pose a serious threat to society.[5] Why such concern? Darwin's theory supplies our increasingly secular culture with its creation story. It has become the primary justification for **naturalism**, the worldview preferred by atheists.

Naturalism sees the universe as a self-contained system of matter and energy that operates by unbroken natural laws. According to naturalism, everything in the universe is the result of chance and necessity, not the purposeful design by God. Thus, if naturalism is true, miracles must have a natural explanation, the Bible cannot be God's inspired Word, and Christianity must be false.

DARWINISM AS AN IDEOLOGY

Young people encounter naturalism in grade school, high school, and in college. Through Darwin's theory, young people are taught that the order and complexity in the world is the result of a blind, material process rather than God's decision to create. Thus, Darwinism serves not merely as a scientific theory but as an ideology meant to account for all of life. Darwinian evolution is used to explain everything from our psychology and economics to telling us why we get sick and why we fall in love.

Darwinism is taken for truth in popular culture. For example, in a *Friends* episode, Phoebe and Ross discuss the merits of Darwinian evolution. Shocked to find that Phoebe rejects it, Ross says, "Uh, excuse me. Evolution is not for you to buy, Phoebe. Evolution is scientific fact, like, like, like the air we breathe, like gravity."

WHY ID MATTERS

Intelligent design is important because it challenges the worldview of naturalism, which needs to explain life as the result of a blind, purposeless, material process (i.e., Darwinian evolution). ID is controversial because it shows that living organisms bear the fingerprint of design. According to ID theorists, the signature of design can be seen throughout life but especially in the information processing of DNA (See Question 8).

Of course, the crucial question is whether ID is true. Darwinists must no longer be able to silence those with whom they disagree. As we will see, ID presents an exciting alternative to Darwinism that not only better accounts for the evidence, but also frees Western culture from its naturalistic straitjacket.

Naturalism is the worldview that sees the universe as a self-contained system of matter and energy that operates by unbroken natural laws.

Ideology is "the body of doctrine, myth, belief, etc., that guides an individual, social movement, institution, class, or large group."[6]

Is Darwinism Scientific Fact?

In the debate over ID and Darwinian evolution, Darwinists proclaim that, in biological origins, they are the true scientists and ID is merely religion masquerading as science. In fact, ID falls squarely within the information and engineering sciences, whereas the Darwinists' inflated claim for the power of natural selection is itself an article of speculative faith.

Natural selection is the hub of Darwin's theory. If Darwin had merely asserted that natural selection accounts for how organisms adapt to changing environmental conditions, that would have been fine. Finch beaks do get thicker and harder during droughts when seeds are harder to crack open. Insects develop insecticide resistance when farmers use toxic chemicals to try to control them. And bacteria develop resistance to antibiotics.

But if finch beak variation, insecticide resistance, and antibiotic resistance were all Darwin's theory attempted to explain, Darwin wouldn't be famous. Instead, Darwin's theory of natural selection is supposed to explain how we got finch beaks (and finches), insects, and bacteria in the first place. If Darwin's theory could do that, he would be justifiably famous. But the evidence for the creative power of natural selection to produce such biological forms is nil. The evidence shows small changes modifying one thing into the same sort of thing; it does not show radical changes transforming one thing into a completely different thing.

Many scientists glimpse the bankruptcy of Darwinism even though they may not be ready to embrace ID. "We should reject, as a matter of principle, the substitution of intelligent design for the dialogue of chance and necessity," writes cell biologist Franklin Harold. Yet he immediately adds, "but we must concede that there are presently no detailed Darwinian accounts of the evolution of any biochemical system, only a variety of wishful speculations."[7]

Natural selection has been shown effective only at producing small-scale evolutionary changes—in other words, microevolution. Microevolutionary change is scarcely noticeable, like moths changing color or size. It is a huge and unwarranted extrapolation to proclaim that natural selection can account for large-scale evolutionary changes—in other words, macroevolution. Macroevolutionary change is profound and radical, like bacteria changing into moths.

The macroevolutionary theory of natural selection lacks all evidence. Even what scant evidence there is for macroevolution does nothing to suggest that natural selection is its cause. Science is about following evidence where it leads. It is not about making stuff up in spite of evidence. It flies in the face of science for Darwinists to proclaim that natural selection evolved complex biological structures. The absence of evidence for such claims is overwhelming.

Natural selection is the process by which nature "selects" the fittest organisms (stronger, quicker, and healthier) to survive and produce offspring.

© Rose Publishing, Inc.

Is ID Science?

Darwinists label ID "non-scientific." But there is no good reason for denying ID scientific status. After all, many scientific disciplines (e.g., archaeology, forensic science, and the Search for Extraterrestrial Intelligence) rely upon detecting the work of intelligence. For instance, when an archaeologist finds an odd shaped rock, she has two general options: (1) it was the result of natural forces (wind, erosion, etc.); or (2) it was intelligently designed. Based upon physical markings alone, archaeologists can often determine which explanation is best. ID theorists apply the same scientific reasoning to the natural world.

METHODOLOGICAL NATURALISM

Some critics reject ID because of a rule known as **methodological naturalism**, which limits science to purely material explanations. Methodological naturalists do not necessarily assume that nature is all that exists; but for the sake of scientific investigation, they say, one can only appeal to unintelligent causes, such as wind, erosion, and the forces of nature. How could we know that the world is the result of entirely natural causes before we begin the investigation? We would rightly be suspicious of a forensic scientist who begins a homicide investigation by only considering natural causes. Science should be open to both natural and intelligent causes, and thus be able to follow the evidence wherever it leads.

Methodological Naturalism: Science is the search for naturalistic explanations of the world.

Historical Definition: Science is the search for the truth of the natural world.

THREE COMMON OBJECTIONS TO ID AS SCIENCE

(1) **Scientific claims must deal with things that are observable, whereas the Designer is unobservable.**
Actually, scientists regularly propose theoretical entities that are unobservable to explain observable phenomena. The Designer of intelligent design is an information source whose activity is as readily the subject of mathematical models and predictions as any physical theory about unobservable entities such as superstrings, dark matter, or multiple universes.[8]

(2) **Science cannot appeal to a Designer because that leaves the origin of the Designer unexplained.**
This is false. For instance, archaeologists regularly conclude that an object was designed, even if they are unaware of the origin of the designer. If every explanation needed a further explanation, then we couldn't explain anything.

(3) **Scientific claims must be testable, but design is supposed to be untestable.**
Critics claim that ID is untestable, but then, they frequently also claim that ID is false. One cannot say, "Design is not testable," and then turn around and say, "Design has been tested and proven false!" A hypothesis cannot be both untestable and tested. In fact, ID has been tested and confirmed across a wide range of disciplines.[9]

What is Irreducible Complexity?

© Felix Möckel

Charles Darwin offered a test for his theory of evolution. In *The Origin of Species* he said, "If it could be demonstrated that any complex organ existed, which could not possibly have been formed by numerous, successive, slight modifications, my theory would absolutely break down."[10] Since Darwinian evolution holds that all complex biological organisms in nature emerged through the step-by-step process of natural selection acting on random mutation, the discovery of a system that could not have formed in this manner would disprove the theory.

TESTING DARWINISM

In 1996, biochemist Michael Behe put Darwin's theory to the test. In his book *Darwin's Black Box*, Behe highlighted certain biological systems in the molecular world that are unlikely to have formed through "numerous, successive, slight modifications," as Darwin's theory requires. Behe introduced the concept of **irreducible complexity**, which describes a system composed of multiple, interworking parts, each required for function. Remove one part, and the entire system fails.

Irreducible complexity is easily understood by considering a mousetrap. Standard mousetraps have multiple, interdependent parts—a wooden platform, a metal bar, a spring, a catch, and a hammer—each of which is necessary for a functioning mousetrap. To catch mice, all the parts must be in the right place at the right time. If one part is missing, the entire system ceases to work.

An irreducibly complex system (such as the mousetrap) is unlikely to emerge suddenly because, as Darwin insisted, evolution is a gradual process. He famously said that natural selection "can *never take a leap*, but must advance by the shortest and slowest steps."[11] An irreducibly complex system cannot simply pop into existence for that would suggest something besides natural selection. Furthermore, evolution could not develop such a system through "numerous, successive, slight modifications" because any simpler system would lack the parts to function, and, therefore, have no reason to exist.

IRREDUCIBLE COMPLEXITY IN NATURE

Behe's controversial claim is that irreducibly complex biological systems exist in nature and refute Darwinism. His most famous example is the bacterial flagellum, a whip-like tail that propels certain bacteria through their watery environment. Harvard scientist Howard Berg called it the most efficient motor in the universe. The flagellum can spin up to 100,000 rpm and change direction in a quarter turn. Like a mousetrap, the flagellum has multiple inter-working parts (at least nine), each of which is necessary for function.

There are no detailed, step-by-step Darwinian accounts for the emergence of the bacterial flagellum or any other irreducibly complex biological system found in nature. Yet we do know that intelligent beings can produce such systems. Molecular machines such as the bacterial flagellum are best understood as the product of intelligent design.

Can Darwinism Explain Life's Origin?

In an 1871 letter to Joseph Hooker, Darwin surmised that life may have begun with chemical reactions in a "warm little pond." Since the cell seemed unremarkable through the microscope of his day, Darwin believed it was rather simple, without order or design. Evolutionary biologists of the late 1800s believed the cell was like a glob of jelly that could easily be constructed through the combination of simple chemicals.

Yet the discovery of the electron microscope in the 1930s completely transformed our understanding of the cell. Scientists now think of the cell as an automated city. The scientific literature is full of comparisons between the cell and modern engineering. In fact, nearly every feature of our own advanced technology can be found in the cell. Examples include transportation, communication, waste management, and defense.

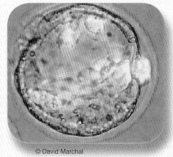
© David Marchal

Given what we have learned about the complexity of the cell, it should come as no surprise that naturalistic origin-of-life research is at a complete standstill. Harvard Chemist George Whitesides confessed that he has "no idea" [12] about the origin of life. Biologist Franklin Harold admits that the origin of life is one of the "unsolved mysteries in science."[13]

Nevertheless, scientists have three key strategies for explaining the cell apart from design:

1. Chemical Evolution: Can life emerge via chemical reactions? Different experiments have attempted to simulate the early conditions of life on Earth to see if life emerges naturally. While such experiments have generated amino acids (the building blocks of protein), none have produced life (the simplest of which being the cell).

2. Self-organization: Does matter have the inherent capacity to organize itself into life? While natural process can produce simple specified structures (such as ice crystals or ripples in the sand), nature cannot generate structures that are both specified and complex (such as the message "I Love Mary" or the information content of DNA). Dean Kenyon, one of the original proponents of self-organization, has since abandoned his theory for ID.

3. Panspermia: Could life have begun elsewhere in the universe and been seeded on Earth? Some scientists believe life "rode" to Earth on the back of meteorites (*undirected panspermia*), and others believe Earth was seeded with life by aliens (*directed panspermia*). These proposals only address how life got to Earth, not its origin. The fact that scientists seriously entertain panspermia illustrates a powerful point: naturalistic origin-of-life research is at a complete standstill.

Where Does Biological Information Come From?

In 2004, leading atheistic philosopher Antony Flew shocked the academic world when he announced that he had changed his mind about God. He cited the information content of DNA as one of the key reasons for his conversion. DNA provides one of the best arguments for intelligent design.

In a widely cited speech, Nobel laureate David Baltimore remarked, "Modern biology is a science of information." With the discovery of the structure of DNA in 1953, scientists realized that the information for encoding proteins is carried in four genetic bases—guanine (G), adenine (A), thymine (T), and cytosine (C). These four bases function like letters of an alphabet, which is why biologists commonly refer to DNA, RNA and proteins as carriers of "information."

The information-storage capacity of DNA far surpasses human technology. Molecular biologist Michael Denton notes that, for all the different types of organisms that have ever existed, the necessary information in their DNA for the construction of their proteins "could be held in a teaspoon and there would still be room left for all the information in every book ever written."[14] But DNA not only stores information, it also processes it. Hence Bill Gates compares DNA to a computer program, though far more advanced than any software humans have invented.[15]

The challenge for origin-of-life researchers is to explain how the information (specified complexity) in living organisms could arise apart from intelligent causation. There is currently no working naturalistic theory for the origin of life. Scientists regularly claim that a solution is at hand, but details are lacking. On their own, natural forces are simply incapable of generating information.

A SOLUTION

By contrast, ID offers a solution that can explain the information content of DNA. Imagine you are walking on the beach and notice a message, "John loves Mary," inscribed in the sand. What would you conclude? Since natural causes (wind, water, and erosion) would be out of the question, you would likely believe that it was the product of design. Information points to a mind.

"Ordinary experience tells us that information, such as a book or computer program, arises from a mind, such as that of an author or computer programmer. The words in a book point beyond themselves to a mind who purposefully arranged them into a meaningful sequence. Just as the information in a book points to an author and computer code points to a programmer, the information content of organisms points to an information source, an intelligent designer."[16]

© Setixela

Is the Universe Designed?

Imagine you discover an abandoned cabin in the mountains. As you approach the cabin, you notice something strange. Your favorite meal is cooking in the oven, the TV is turned on to your favorite program, and all your favorite books, DVDs, and video games are lying on the table. What would you conclude? The best explanation would clearly be that someone was expecting your arrival. Scientists have recently learned that the universe is much like this cabin—it's crafted uniquely for us.

There are nineteen known physical laws that must each be exquisitely fine-tuned for life—not just life on Earth, but for the existence of any complex life. Examples of these include the law of gravity, the strong nuclear force, and the electromagnetic force. The slightest change in any of these and the universe becomes uninhabitable for complex life.

For instance, if the initial mass of the universe had varied by any more than a single grain of table salt, the universe would not exist. The universe either could not have expanded, or it would have expanded so rapidly that it would spread out to nothingness almost immediately.[17] As Goldilocks would say, the universe is "just right" for life.

Design is also apparent in the multiple factors that must be just right for a habitable planet. Life cannot flourish anywhere in the universe. In fact, most places are extremely hostile to life. Consider a few examples:

1. **Life requires the right type of galaxy.** Of the three types of galaxies, only spiral galaxies can support life.

2. **Life requires the right location in the galaxy.** Earth is situated in a unique location in the Milky Way to avoid harmful radiation.

3. **Life requires the right type of star.** While most stars are too large, too luminous, or too unstable to support life, our Sun is just right.

4. **Life must have the right relationship to its host star.** If Earth's distance from the sun varied even slightly, water would either freeze or evaporate, rendering Earth uninhabitable for complex life.

5. **Life needs surrounding planets for protection.** Large surrounding bodies (such as Jupiter or Uranus) are needed as protection from incoming comets.

6. **Life requires the right type of moon.** To be habitable, Earth needs a moon of a certain size and distance. The moon creates a stable, life-friendly environment by stabilizing Earth's tilt.

Many other factors are needed for a habitable planet. But the point should be clear—*the universe as a whole and Earth in particular are just right for life*. The best explanation for why the universe is just right for life is that an Intelligent Designer made it that way.

What About Bad Design and Evil?

BAD DESIGN

Critics of intelligent design point out cases of supposedly bad design in nature and use these to argue against the very existence of design. In their view, bad design means no design—period.

The classic formulation of this criticism can be found in Stephen Jay Gould's *The Panda's Thumb*: "If God had designed a beautiful machine to reflect his wisdom and power, surely he would not have used a collection of parts generally fashioned for other purposes.... Odd arrangements and funny solutions are the proof of evolution—paths that a sensible God would never tread but that a natural process, constrained by history, follows perforce."[18]

© Fernando Revilla

Gould here is finding fault with the "panda's thumb," a bony extrusion that helps the giant panda strip bamboo of its hard exterior to make it edible. But is this really a case of bad design? In fact, the panda's thumb seems an extremely efficient instrument for stripping bamboo. How does Gould know what a "sensible God" would do, especially since he offers no design improvement on the panda's thumb? In the vast majority of cases where Darwinists find fault with biological design, good functional reasons exist for the design in question and no detailed proposal exists for improving it.

EVIL DESIGN

A more troubling challenge to design, however, comes from natural evil. Nature contains disease, decay, and death. It contains parasites that seem ingeniously and malevolently designed to harm other organisms. Troubled by such perversity in nature, Darwin wrote, "I cannot persuade myself that a beneficent and omnipotent God would have designedly created the Ichneumonidae [certain parasitic wasps] with the express intention of their feeding within the living bodies of Caterpillars."[19]

This nasty little creature first injects a caterpillar with an anaesthetic to put it to sleep and then deposits its eggs inside it. When the eggs hatch, they carefully eat the caterpillar, sparing the vital organs so that they have a fresh supply of food till the caterpillar dies.

In responding to the charge of evil design, we need to be clear about two things. First, the evilness of design does not refute the reality of design. It may raise questions about the morality of the designer. But it cannot disprove design as such, which can be detected through the methods of science. Second, as Christians, we believe that the evil design that we see in nature does not represent God's original design-plan for creation but rather its corruption through the sin of humanity.

Christianity has always taught that the world we inhabit is not the world God originally intended. The natural evil we see around us (such as sickness, parasites, and death) as well as the moral evil we inflict on each other (such as theft, murder, and torture) are not what God wanted for us from the start but came upon us through sin.[20]

Quick Response Guide to Common Objections[21]

OBJECTION #1: ID makes no predictions.

RESPONSE: ID predicts that there should be structures beyond the reach of chance-based Darwinian mechanisms. And there are (for example, the bacterial flagellum).

OBJECTION #2: ID is religiously motivated.

RESPONSE: ID constructs a scientific case against Darwinian evolution. The motivation of its advocates is irrelevant. Stephen Hawking hopes his work in physics will help us understand the mind of God. Steven Weinberg hopes his work in physics will help to destroy religion. Do their motivations invalidate their science? Of course not.

OBJECTION #3: ID argues from ignorance.

RESPONSE: ID doesn't just identify holes in Darwinian evolution, but it also explores positive features of design present in biological systems, such as the specified complexity in DNA and the molecular machinery inside cells.

OBJECTION #4: ID violates the scientific consensus.

RESPONSE: So did Copernicus, Galileo, Kepler, Newton, and even Darwin himself! The point of science is not to protect a consensus but to provide an accurate understanding of the universe, and that requires a readiness to break with consensus.

OBJECTION #5: ID is a science-stopper.

RESPONSE: ID encourages science in ways that Darwinism hinders. Darwinism, for example, predicts that a lot of DNA is junk. Intelligent design encourages the ongoing search for function in DNA. In this regard, ID has been vindicated over Darwinism. ID keeps Darwinism honest. It therefore can't be a science-stopper.

OBJECTION #6: ID violates the scientific method.

RESPONSE: The scientific method tests hypotheses in light of evidence. ID does this too. For example, it tests the hypothesis that irreducibly complex systems are designed by determining whether Darwinian evolutionary mechanisms are capable of producing them.

OBJECTION #7: Imperfection in living things counts against design.

RESPONSE: Imperfection speaks to the quality of design, not to its reality. No one seriously thinks that design must be perfect to be detectable. Because ecological balance demands that all life forms must die and be recycled, some imperfection is unavoidable.

OBJECTION #8: ID is Bible-based.

RESPONSE: While the findings of ID are consistent with the Bible, the evidence for design comes from cosmology, physics, chemistry, biology, information theory, and other scientific disciplines.

OBJECTION #9: No peer-reviewed journal articles supporting ID exist.

RESPONSE: Although articles supporting ID have difficulty gaining a fair hearing, a growing number of peer-reviewed journal articles and books supporting design do in fact exist (see www.discovery.org/a/2640).

OBJECTION #10: No credible scholars support ID.

RESPONSE: University of Georgia professor Henry Schaefer III, one of the most widely cited chemists in the world with over 1,000 publications, supports ID. So do other prominent scientists at places like Princeton, USC, and Baylor.

Notes

1 William Paley, *Natural Theology: Or Evidences of the Existence and Attributes of the Deity Collected from the Appearances of Nature*, reprinted (Boston: Gould and Lincoln, 1852 [1802]).

2 Francisco J. Ayala, *Darwin's Gift to Science and Religion* (Washington, D.C.: Joseph Henry Press, 2007), 42.

3 See William A. Dembski & Sean McDowell, *Understanding Intelligent Design* (Eugene, OR: Harvest House, 2008).

4 William Dembski, *The Design Inference* (Cambridge: Cambridge University Press, 1998), chs. 2 and 7.

5 Daniel C. Dennett, *Darwin's Dangerous Idea: Evolution and the Meaning of Life* (New York: Simon & Schuster, 1995), 519.

6 http://dictionary.reference.com/browse/ideology (last viewed April 2, 2009).

7 Franklin Harold, *The Way of the Cell* (Oxford: Oxford University Press, 2001), 205.

8 For the role of the mathematical theory of information in characterizing the information-generating properties of the Designer, go to www.evoinfo.org (last accessed April 14, 2009).

9 William Dembski and Jonathan Wells, *The Design of Life: Discovering Signs of Intelligence in Biological Systems* (Dallas: Foundation for Thought and Ethics, 2008); Guillermo Gonzalez and Jay W. Richards, *The Privileged Planet: How Our Place in the Cosmos Is Designed for Discovery* (Washington, DC: Regnery, 2004).

10 Charles Darwin, *On the Origin of Species*, facsimile 1st ed. (1859; reprinted Cambridge, Mass.: Harvard University Press, 1964), 189.

11 Ibid, 194, emphasis added.

12 George M. Whitesides, "Revolutions in Chemistry" (Priestly Medalist address), *Chemical & Engineering News* 85(13) (March 26, 2007): 12–17.

13 Franklin Harold, *The Way of the Cell: Molecules, Organisms, and the Order of Life* (New York: Oxford University Press, 2001), 235.

14 Michael Denton, *Evolution: A Theory in Crisis* (Chevy Chase, MD: Adler and Adler, 1986), 334.

15 Bill Gates, *The Road Ahead* (Boulder, Colo.: Blue Penguin, 1996), 228.

16 See William A. Dembski & Sean McDowell, *Understanding Intelligent Design* (Eugene, OR: Harvest House, 2008), 81-82.

17 Mark Whorton & Hill Roberts, *Holman QuickSource Guide to Understanding Creation* (Nashville, TN: 2008), 308.

18 Stephen Jay Gould, *The Panda's Thumb* (New York: Norton, 1980), pp. 20-21.

19 Charles Darwin, *The Correspondence of Charles Darwin* 8, 1860 (Cambridge: Cambridge University Press, 1993), 224.

20 William A. Dembski, *The End of Christianity: Finding a Good God in an Evil World* (Nashville: Broadman and Holman, 2009), in press. To understand how sin could open the door to the evils we now experience is the subject of William Dembski's *The End of Christianity*.

21 Taken directly from William A. Dembski & Sean McDowell, *Understanding Intelligent Design* (Eugene, OR: Harvest House, 2008), 190-92.

Authors: William Dembski, PhD, has authored numerous books on intelligent design. He teaches at Southwestern Baptist Theological Seminary in Ft. Worth, Texas.

Sean McDowell, MA, is a teacher, speaker, and is the co-author of *Understanding Intelligent Design*. He blogs regularly at www.seanmcdowell.org.

Myths about God's Existence

Myth: There's no evidence for God's existence.

Myth: Humans decide what is right and wrong.

Myth: A good God can't exist because evil exists.

Myth: There's no ultimate meaning in life.

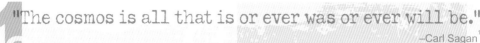

"The cosmos is all that is or ever was or ever will be."

–Carl Sagan[1]

What Are Atheism and Agnosticism?

Atheism Claims...

Atheism disbelieves in the existence of God. The universe—matter—is all that exists. The universe operates via natural physical laws. Any event that may seem supernatural is really a natural occurrence. Miracles do not occur. The reality of evil, the apparent purposelessness of life, the seeming randomness of the universe, and the fact of evolution all argue against the existence of God. Christianity is false. The Bible is an error-filled book of flawed human origin. Jesus, if he even existed, performed no miracles, did not rise from the dead, and was not God.

Agnosticism Claims...

Agnosticism asserts that God may or may not exist. Since it is impossible to prove the existence or non-existence of God, we just don't know if God exists or not. A *universal*, *hard* or *aggressive* agnostic denies that anyone can answer the question of God. The only wise course of action is to reserve judgment and remain skeptical. A *local*, *soft* or *modest* agnostic claims that the evidence for or against God is not enough to warrant a decision. Therefore, such an agnostic remains undecided.

The Bible Teaches...

God exists and has chosen to reveal himself through creation, moral conscience, and the Bible.

From these sources of revelation, Christians conclude that God exists beyond the world (transcendent), yet is active in creation (immanent), created the world out of nothing (*ex nihilo*), is all powerful (omnipotent), all knowing (omniscient), ever present (omnipresent), and all loving (omnibenevolent).

The natural universe is not all that exists. Since God exists, miracles are possible.

The case for biblical Christianity as the best explanation of reality includes, but is not limited to: historical evidence, archaeology, philosophical integrity, and eyewitness testimony.

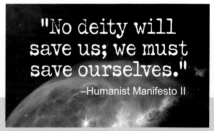

"No deity will save us; we must save ourselves."

–Humanist Manifesto II

You Should Also Know...

• The word "atheist" comes from the Greek *a*, meaning "not" or "no," and *theos*, meaning "God." An atheist embraces a belief system that says "not God." The word "agnostic" is derived from the Greek *gnosis* ("knowledge") and literally means "no knowledge."

• Modern atheism emerged as a formal philosophy in the 19th century.

Many contemporary atheists prefer to be called humanists.

• The atheist says that nothing exists outside of the known physical universe. Agnosticism asserts that definite knowledge about God is unattainable. But the assertion, "No one can really know anything for sure about God," is also a definitive statement regarding what one knows about God.

2

"The heavens declare the glory of God."
—Psalm 19:1

Q: What Can We Know About the Existence of God?

Atheism Claims...

Many atheists have a high regard for reason with a bias toward empiricism (that which can be measured by the senses). Since God cannot be measured and quantified, there is no viable evidence for his existence. Science and philosophical reasoning argue against the existence of God. Since evolution explains human origins, God is unnecessary. If the universe is eternal or can be shown to have come into existence spontaneously and by chance, then God is also unnecessary.

Agnosticism Claims...

Agnostics are skeptical of reason and all other systems of knowing. As a result, they shy away from claiming certain knowledge about reality or God. One cannot or does not know anything for certain; therefore one cannot or does not know if God exists. Although agnostics claim not to know whether God exists, many function as atheists.

> "... the most plausible answer to the question of why something exists rather than nothing is that God exists."
> —William Lane Craig, *Reasonable Faith*

You Should Also Know...

While atheists in particular exalt human reason and the capacity to interpret reality scientifically, the very nature of reason is in question if God does not exist. If humans are the products of evolutionary chance, why should our reasoning abilities be trusted?

Arguments for the existence of God:

A: The Bible Teaches...

Christianity has a high regard for reason, but recognizes its limitations in defining a God who is by nature unlimited. The God of the Bible has revealed much about himself that is conclusively knowable. God reveals himself through creation, communication through his Word, and conscience.

Creation: Our complex universe shows evidence of a Creator. Sensory input from the physical world provides knowledge through which we know God. Sometimes called *general revelation*, these are things God reveals about himself through nature to everyone (Romans 1:20).

Communication: The content of the *Bible* gives evidence of divine origin. This communication is called *special revelation*; these are the things God told to specific people at specific times in history.

Conscience: The moral law written on human *conscience* points to a Moral Lawgiver (Romans 2:14–15).

Cosmological argument[2]
- Everything that had a beginning has a cause.
- The universe had a beginning.
- Therefore, the universe had a cause.

Design argument[3]
- Every design has a designer.
- The universe—and life—has highly complex design.
- Therefore, there is a Great Designer.

Moral argument[4]
- Moral laws require a lawgiver.
- Absolute moral laws exist.
- Therefore, there is an absolute Moral Lawgiver.

"In the beginning God created

What Can We Know About Right and Wrong?

Atheism Claims...

Since God does not exist, neither do transcendent moral absolutes. Morality is relative to one's personal perspective or cultural norms. There may be some widely accepted and enduring values, perhaps to aid in our survival. Because values do not come from God, they must originate with human beings.

An individual's judgment or the decision of the majority determines societal values. Some atheists favor utilitarian ethics, where "the good" is what is best for the greatest number of people over the long run.

Making God the source of morality is flawed. If God simply declares something good or bad, his decision seems arbitrary, but if God merely acknowledges the good that already exists, God seems unnecessary or less than the good.

Agnosticism Claims...

Depending on the individual agnostic, there are various views of morality. Some will apply their agnosticism to the question of ethics. As a result, ethics are also unknowable; however, these kinds of agnostics would approve of a social contract form of ethics.

In order for society to properly function, it is generally in everyone's best interests to go along with culturally accepted moral standards.

The Bible Teaches...

Right and wrong exist, and the fact of their existence is rooted in God's nature. These transcendent laws are both written on the hearts of all people, are known in one's moral conscience (Romans 2:15) and are revealed by God in the Bible.

A study of numerous cultures shows an amazing similarity about peoples' regard for right and wrong. While there is room for some cultural variation, what these cultures agree on is greater than what they disagree about.[5]

Because a righteous God exists, morality is *absolute*, not *relative*. Since morality is based on God's character rather than on human opinion, actions may be identified as good or evil. God is the "measuring stick" for determining right and wrong.

> "What is moral is what you feel good after, and what is immoral is what you feel bad after."
> —Ernest Hemingway,
> *Death in the Afternoon*

You Should Also Know...

Atheism claims that if moral values exist, they must have their source in human beings. But atheists believe human beings are products of *impersonal* chance and time. However, moral values dictate *personal* behavior between personal beings. How is it that an impersonal universe could result in personal morality?

The atheistic belief that either 1) God is arbitrary in his insistence that something is good, or 2) good is greater than God, is false. Values are rooted in God's perfect nature. Since this is the case, standards of right and wrong flow naturally from God. Atheists have no basis for saying evil exists. For how can one know something is unjust unless one knows a standard of justice by which to pronounce it unjust?

the eavens and the earth." –Genesis 1:1

4 Is Belief in God Compatible with Science?

Atheism Claims...

If Christians can claim that God had no beginning, then atheists can claim that what makes up the universe is uncaused and eternal. Even if the universe had a beginning, this does not mean that God caused it. Evolution, over time and chance, explains human origins, not God.

Science has made God unnecessary. As humanity progresses and increases in scientific knowledge, questions that were once answered by appealing to religion and God are solved by science. God is not needed to fill in the gaps.

Agnosticism Claims...

While agnostics by definition do not claim to know whether or not God exists, they tend to side with atheists when reconciling science and religion. If God exists, he must be much less than the Christian view of God, since the universe could have been designed better. Instead, there is evidence of flawed biological design, death and decay, viciousness in the animal world, and seemingly no purpose to the universe. If there is a God, he must be limited, distant, or wicked.

The Bible Teaches...

All truth is God's truth. Christianity welcomes scientific investigation. God has given us a vast amount of material to explore and understand.

Christians can agree with microevolution—moderate changes within certain types of life such as dogs and cats. Macroevolution, however, claims large-scale changes such as the random development of new structures like wings, new organs like lungs, and new body plans. The lack of transitional forms in the fossil record combined with signs of the abrupt appearance of fully-formed creatures argues against macroevolution. Many credible scientists admit that a viable "missing link" has yet to be found, even though Darwin expected many to be found.

The evidence can be explained by the existence of a Designer who created the universe *ex nihilo* at a specific point in time. Evidence shows that complex design in living things requires the involvement of a Designer.

You Should Also Know...

Science has *not* made God unnecessary. As C.S. Lewis wrote: "Supposing science ever became complete so that it knew every single thing in the whole universe. Is it not plain that the questions, 'Why is there a universe?' 'Why does it go on as it does?' 'Has it any meaning?' would remain just as they were?"[6]

Claiming the universe had a beginning is not outmoded. Scientists Stephen Hawking and Roger Penrose admit "… almost everyone now believes that the universe, and time itself, had a beginning at the big bang."[7]

"It is absolutely safe to say that if you meet somebody who claims not to believe in evolution, that person is ignorant, stupid, or insane (or wicked, but I'd rather not consider that)."

–Richard Dawkins[8]

Is There Scientific Evidence Supporting Belief in God?

Atheism Claims...

Atheists reject the validity of scientific evidence for the existence of God. Since atheists are naturalists, miracles are rejected, including supernatural elements of the Bible. Miracles are either defined out of existence or considered contrary to the scientific method. If anything, science offers evidence *against* the existence of God such as macroevolution and imperfections in biological systems. Why would an all-powerful God create flawed designs?

Agnosticism Claims...

Agnostics question the possibility that science can prove or disprove the existence of God. Some agnostics would take a harder stance, arguing that since God is unknowable, the question of what science can prove or disprove in this regard is irrelevant. Other agnostics are open to various lines of evidence, but doubt that science can help arrive at a Creator. Others believe that since macroevolution is assumed to be truth rather than theory, the scientific case against God appears formidable.

The Bible Teaches...

God has revealed himself—"For since the creation of the world God's invisible qualities—his eternal power and divine nature—have been clearly seen, being understood from what has been made, so that men are without excuse" (Romans 1:20).

Christians have contributed significantly to the development of science as a field of study because of interest in learning about God's creation.

The anthropic ("man-centered") principle argues that the universe shows signs that it is so finely tuned to support human life that it cannot be an accident that human life exists. Even slight variations in seemingly inconsequential factors (such as rotation speed, temperature, atmosphere, the tilt of the earth) would be catastrophic.

These lines of evidence point to the existence of a Designer who is intelligent and powerful.

You Should Also Know...

The question of whether scientific evidence can support the existence of God requires an assessment of what science is dealing with and what it can and cannot do. *Operation science* studies the present, is repeatable, and examines how things work. It deals with the way things normally operate. However, origin events were not observed and cannot be repeated. *Origin science,* therefore, operates more like *forensic science,* by which the past is reconstructed on the basis of evidence that remains in the present.

"Is there any dogma more unsupported by the facts than from the scientist who stands up and says, "I know there is no God"? Science is woefully unsuited to ask the question of God in the first place."

–Francis Collins, United States' top geneticist[9]

If God is Good, Why Is There Evil?

Atheism Claims...

Theists claim that God is all powerful and all loving. But evil exists both morally, in what people do, and naturally in earthquakes, floods, hurricanes, and more. How could a loving God allow evil?

An absolutely good God must have a good purpose for everything, so if evil exists, there cannot be an absolutely good God. The reality of evil demonstrates that either there is no God or he is not the good God of theism and, therefore, not worthy of worship.

Agnosticism Claims...

Because we do not know reality conclusively, it is impossible to say that evil exists. What seems evil may be only incomplete knowledge. The judgment that something is evil may simply be a judgment made with no basis in reality. If God exists and has attributes like those described by the Bible, then it seems inconsistent for evil and suffering to exist.

The Bible Teaches...

A good God created human beings with the power of free will to choose between good and evil. Abuse of free choice (moral evil) is explained by the bad choices of free creatures. Without freedom, people would be robots. They could not choose to love or to respond to love. Therefore, God has allowed evil to exist, but people are responsible for choosing it.

Natural evil (natural disaster) was also introduced into the physical world as a consequence of bad choices from Adam on. We live in a fallen world—"the whole creation has been groaning" (Romans 8:22).

The dilemma: Either God is sovereign and he has allowed evil for a good purpose, or God is not sovereign and evil is a power equal with God. The Bible shows that the second option is incorrect, and that God did, indeed, allow evil for a greater good. In other words, this is not the best *world*, but the best *way* to the best possible world.

You Should Also Know...

Without an objective standard of right and wrong, how can atheists and agnostics call anything "evil"? Atheists (and most agnostics) assume that evil exists and point to injustices as evidence against God. But "evil" and "injustice" are concepts that require the existence of a standard. If God does not exist, where does this standard come from?

Evil is parasitic—it only exists as a negation of good, not as a thing itself. God did not create evil, but by creating free creatures God left open the possibility of the choice of evil. God is responsible for the *fact* of freedom, but not the *acts* of freedom. If God were to destroy all evil now, no one would exist. God would have to destroy both actual and potential evil; this means he would have to destroy all free will.

"You are not a God who takes pleasure in evil ..." –Psalm 5:4

What about All the Evil Done in the Name of God?

Atheism Claims...

Religion has done more harm than good. Christianity is responsible for countless atrocities throughout history including the Crusades, the Salem witch trials, the Inquisition, the KKK, and more.

What God would allow all this evil to be done in his name? The history of the world clearly shows that wherever religion is present, there is sure to be evil done in God's name. This is evidence that God does not exist.

Agnosticism Claims...

While it can't be known whether or not God exists, religious history shows a pattern of evil done in the name of God, usually by Christians.

If everyone were agnostic, the world would be a safer place. There would be no need for different religions to war against one another or against atheists and agnostics. The idea of God appears to be more trouble than it's worth.

The Bible Teaches...

While it is true that some people claiming to be Christian have committed atrocities in the name of God, this does not mean that God does not exist. Sometimes evil done in the name of God is done by misguided Christians, and sometimes they are the acts of "cultural" Christians who do not truly follow God's rules for living.

Evil done in the name of God is not in line with the teachings of Jesus. If everyone followed the teachings of Christ correctly, no evil would be done in the name of God.

Jesus taught people to love God and their neighbors (Matthew 22:37–40), as well as what has become known as the Golden Rule: "So in everything, do to others what you would have them do to you" (Matthew 7:12). Evil done in the name of God does not represent true Christianity.

> "'A loving God' could not possibly be the author of the horrors we have been describing ... it is obvious that there cannot be a loving God."
> —Charles Templeton, *Farewell to God*

You Should Also Know...

Christians could point to all the atrocities done in the name of atheistic worldviews such as Communism. In China alone the 20th century witnessed some 65 million deaths as a result of a belief system based on atheism. Logically, however, this does not mean that atheism is false. Likewise, pointing to atrocities done in the name of God does not mean Christianity is false. If anything, evil in the world supports the Christian belief that everyone has a bent toward selfishness and egotism—what the Bible calls "sin." Moreover, when atheists and agnostics argue against God on the basis of evil done in his name, they acknowledge the reality of standards of good and evil, something they cannot rationally do based on atheistic beliefs.

Christians have founded hospitals, institutions of higher learning, and humanitarian organizations in order to help fellow human beings whom they realize are made in the image of God and, therefore, are inherently valuable. Love, not hate, is the foundation of Christian ethics.

"All Scripture is God-breathed..." –2 Timothy 3:16

Is the Bible an Unreliable Collection of Legends?

Atheism Claims...

The Bible is an unreliable book. It is at best irrelevant, possibly heavily rewritten, and at worst is subversive and dangerous. Since the Bible includes miracles, it can't be right. It was written at a simpler time when people were more easily fooled. If Jesus ever existed, the Bible was put together long after he died, thereby allowing his followers to make up whatever they wanted. Even Christian scholars admit that we don't have the original Bible manuscripts. How can we know whether anything written about Jesus is true? The Bible is full of contradictions and scientific errors.

Agnosticism Claims...

The Bible may contain some great literature, but there is no way to know for sure whether what it records really happened or not. Christians have to take it on faith. Although it can't be known for certain whether or not the Bible is true, based on the available evidence the Bible appears to be unreliable. It contains errors, contradicts science, and is full of "miracles."

The Bible Teaches...

The Bible records real events that took place in real historical settings, about real people, and that tell about real miracles. The Bible mentions historically verifiable facts, supported by thousands of archaeological discoveries. Many inscriptions, archaeological objects, and excavations of ancient cities verify the Bible's reliability on historical events.[10] The Bible also records that Jesus claimed to be God in the flesh (see Mark 2:5–7; John 8:58; 10:33), something he demonstrated by many miracles and especially by rising from the dead, an event verified by both friends and enemies.

The Bible is God's Word. It was written by men who were inspired and guided by God. The Bible is without error in the original manuscripts.

> "... a mass of fables and traditions, mere mythology."
> –Mark Twain on the Bible

You Should Also Know...

Some portions of the New Testament were written within just 20 years or so of the crucifixion and resurrection of Christ. These portions, such as 1 Corinthians 15, put forth core truths about Christianity. There was no time for legends and myths to develop. Many people who witnessed events during the time of Christ were alive when the New Testament was written and circulated. All ancient works—sacred and secular—were written on very fragile material such as leather or papyrus. Therefore we do not possess the original biblical manuscripts. What we do have are very accurate copies that convey all the essential truths of the originals.

The main reason atheists and some unbelieving scholars reject the Bible is not on the basis of the evidence, but on the basis of anti-supernaturalism. Seeming contradictions are just that—seeming. Bible scholars have offered numerous works answering critics.[11]

"... we can discover no divine purpose

Is There Life after Death?

Atheism Claims...

This life is all there is. Good works or the advancement of human understanding can cause you to leave behind an impression in the memories of others. Immortality in the Christian sense is false. Human beings will not live forever. Once the body dies, there is nothing more. One might say that as the body decays, it will ultimately rejoin the universe and be part of it in some way, but once we die, consciousness as we know it ceases to exist. No heaven or hell awaits us. This life is all we have. There is no need for salvation.

Agnosticism Claims...

No one knows whether or not there is life after death. The best available evidence seems to support naturalism. While a definitive decision can't be made on the question of the afterlife, it seems as though the Christian position is wrong. Science shows we are just material beings. Evidence for life after death is anecdotal. Stories of "near-death experiences" hardly prove that consciousness exists beyond death forever. Salvation is not possible, nor necessary, since this life is probably all there is.

The Bible Teaches...

Human beings are both material and immaterial. After death, we enter an intermediate state until the resurrection of the body occurs. At the time of the final judgment, we will either spend eternity separated from God or in his presence. Although there is evidence for life after death beyond the Bible, the greatest testimony is Jesus Christ. He not only predicted his death and resurrection, but it actually happened in history. At one point more than 500 people saw Jesus alive after his death and resurrection (1 Cor. 15:6).

Salvation is by God's grace, through faith, in Christ alone. Since "man is destined to die once, and after that to face judgment" (Hebrews 9:27), it is critical to choose to live for Christ before death.

"Where, O death, is your victory? Where, O death, is your sting?"
—1 Corinthians 15:55

You Should Also Know...

The mind-body problem is a serious challenge for atheists and agnostics. Whether it is called consciousness, mind, or the soul, there appears to be an immaterial component to human beings. If the material world is all that exists, why does evidence seem to point to an immaterial component to human beings?

Why, for instance, do ideas themselves matter so much to humans? Concepts like freedom, love, justice, humor, and beauty cannot be reduced to the simply material without the loss of these properties. In fact, the very things that make us most human, that set us apart, are these immaterial truths residing in the consciousness. This data is ignored by the materialist or dismissed as irrelevant.

If God exists, the case for immortality (life after death) makes sense, since it is this data, these properties, that mark us in God's image and are eternal.

or providence for the human species." –Humanist Manifesto II

10.

Is There Meaning and Purpose to Life?

Atheism Claims...

In general, atheists believe there is no universal meaning or purpose to life. Some atheists believe there is no apparent purpose to life other than biological determinism (to reproduce and therefore to ensure survival of the species). Others believe that since no god exists, this life is the ultimate purpose and should be maximized or lived in order to advance the race and extend human knowledge. Atheists of the humanistic variety are more hopeful, claiming that we can leave a good legacy to future generations.

Agnosticism Claims...

The purpose of life is either unknowable or nonexistent. Some agnostics are convinced that the universe, including human life, is merely the product of chance and time. In this sense, the Darwinian "survival of the fittest" can be said to provide some purpose—the survival and improvement of the human animal. Other agnostics say there is a longing in them that nothing on earth can satisfy. They sense there must be something more to life—some greater purpose—but they have yet to find conclusive evidence of such a purpose.

A: The Bible Teaches...

Life has meaning and purpose because God exists. History has a purpose because it is guided by the greater purposes of God. Individuals have meaning and purpose. Being created in the image of God (Genesis 1:27), every person is of inherent value, capable of expressing emotion, engaging the intellect, using creativity, and longing for God.

God, as St. Augustine wrote, has made us for himself and "our hearts are restless until they find rest in Thee" [God].[12] Ultimate meaning and purpose is found in a relationship with God, through Christ, that impacts both belief and behavior.

"I have come that they may have life, and have it to the full." –Jesus, John 10:10

You Should Also Know...

The logical outcome of the atheistic worldview is *nihilism*, a philosophy that says nothing in the world has real existence. Ultimately, given atheistic beliefs there is no lasting meaning and purpose to life. Some atheists acknowledge this, while others, such as secular humanists, continue to argue that human life still has purpose even without God. Even famed atheist Bertrand Russell admitted, "Brief and powerless is Man's life; on him and all his race the slow, sure doom falls pitiless and dark ...".[13] Agnostics straddle the fence of decision intellectually, yet remain indecisive. Many live as functional atheists and are closer to nihilism than they think. If a person cannot know whether or not God exists, life may as well be meaningless.

Christianity offers a better way, grounded in the reality of the existence of God. There is a yearning in everyone that only God can fill.

"Christianity, if false, is of no importance, and if true, of infinite importance. The only thing it cannot be is moderately important." —C.S. Lewis

"We have a right to believe whatever we want, but not everything we believe is right."

—Ravi Zacharias

"We trust not because 'a God' exists, but because this God exists."

—C.S. Lewis

"If God exists and we are made in his image we can have real meaning, and we can have real knowledge through what he has communicated to us."

"After I set out to refute Christianity intellectually and couldn't, I came to the conclusion the Bible was true and Jesus Christ was God's Son." —Josh McDowell

—Francis Shaeffer

"How does God rescue the life of the needy from the hands of the wicked? Overwhelmingly, he does it through those who choose to follow him in faith and obedience. He doesn't need our 'help,' but he chooses to use us." —Gary Haugen

"No man knows how bad he is till he has tried very hard to be good." —C.S. Lewis

"God cannot give us a happiness and peace apart from Himself, because it is not there. There is no such thing." —C.S. Lewis

"God is more interested in your future and your relationships than you are." —Billy Graham

Glossary of Atheistic & Agnostic Terms

Agnosticism: Meaning "no knowledge," agnosticism believes the existence of God can neither be proven nor disproven. Many agnostics live as functional atheists.

Apologetics: Reasoned arguments in justification of a theory. Christian apologetics use reason and logic to demonstrate the reliability of Christianity. Apologetics may be positive, such as arguing for the reliability of the Bible, or negative, such as critiquing competing worldviews (see 1 Peter 3:15).

Atheism: The belief that God or gods do not exist. Only matter exists; this worldview is often called naturalism. Atheism has much in common with secular humanism.

Big Bang: A scientific theory that the universe began as an explosion of dense matter.

Cosmological arguments: These kinds of arguments claim that belief in God is reasonable due to the origin and existence of the universe. For example, the *kalam* ("First Cause") cosmological argument states that anything that has a beginning has a cause. Since the universe had a beginning, it must have had a cause. The best explanation for the cause of the universe is God.

Design arguments: Also known as teleological arguments, the basic approach of design arguments is to argue for the existence of God on the basis of design in the universe. Hints of this argument are found in Psalm 19 and Romans 1:20.

Empiricism: Theory that all knowledge comes through experience. Empirical knowledge can be proven through experiment and observation; by extension, the senses may be relied upon to correctly interpret reality.

Ex nihilo: Creation "out of nothing." Christians believe God created the universe *ex nihilo*. Atheists and agnostics generally believe that matter and energy are eternal or that the universe came into existence from nothing and by nothing.

General Revelation: Things God reveals about himself through nature to everyone.

Mind-Body Problem: A problem for atheists because evidence seems to point to an immaterial component to human beings, but the atheistic worldview claims that the material world is all that exists.

Moral/axiological arguments: Moral arguments for the existence of God claim that the existence of moral laws suggests the existence of a transcendent moral lawgiver.

Moral relativism: Belief that morality is relative. Rejecting or doubting the existence of God, atheists and agnostics attempt to ground moral values in human nature, evolutionary processes, social contracts, etc., rather than in a transcendent source.

Naturalism: A worldview that embraces matter as all that exists, thus rejecting anything supernatural including the existence of God and the possibility of miracles.

Nihilism: A philosophy that says nothing in the world has real existence. It is the logical outcome of the atheistic worldview.

Origin Science: The kind of study which attempts to reconstruct the past on the basis of evidence that remains in the present.

Problem of evil: If a good, loving God exists, why is there evil? Theological efforts to reconcile God's attributes with the

Glossary of Atheistic & Agnostic Terms

existence of evil are known as *theodicies*. Many theodicies exist.

Secular humanism: Belief that human beings are basically good, and are capable of living morally and being fulfilled without belief in God or reference to anything divine or supernatural.

Skepticism: Doubt or denial regarding the capacity to arrive at absolute conclusions about knowledge. Skepticism has much in common with agnosticism. Skeptics, however, do not appear skeptical of skepticism, which leads to internal inconsistencies.

Special Revelation: Things God reveals about himself told to specific people at specific times in history.

Supernaturalism: A worldview that believes in not only the existence of the material world, but also the reality of a supernatural realm. Christianity embraces supernaturalism, while atheism rejects it.

Theism: Belief in the existence of God or gods, especially belief in the Judeo-Christian God who created the universe and sustains it and his creatures in a personal way. From the Greek *theos* (God).

Transcendent: Beyond the range of normal or physical human experience.

Worldview: How one views and interprets reality, particularly in relation to the great questions of life.

NOTES:
1 C. Sagan, "Cosmos," 1980.
2 See W. L. Craig, *Does God Exist?*
3 See M. Behe, *Darwin's Black Box*
4 See C.S. Lewis, *Mere Christianity*
5 See C.S. Lewis, appendix to *The Abolition of Man*
6 C.S. Lewis, *Mere Christianity*, p. 32
7 *The Nature of Space and Time* by Stephen Hawking and Roger Penrose (Princeton University Press, 1996), p. 20
8 R. Dawkins, "Signs of Intelligence," NY Times, April 9, 1989, sec. VII, p. 34
9 F. Collins, "The Discover Interview" by D.E. Duncan, *Discover* magazine, February, 2007, p. 75
10 See "Archaeology and the Bible," Rose Publishing
11 See Geisler & Howe, *When Critics Ask*
12 Augustine, *Confessions* 1.1
13 B. Russell, "A Free Man's Worship"

Authors
Norman L. Geisler, M.A., Th.B., Ph.D., is the founder and Dean of Southern Evangelical Seminary and the Veritas Graduate School of Apologetics. He is author of numerous books on apologetics and theology, many of which are considered "standard texts" in Christian colleges throughout the world.
Alex McFarland, M.A., is the president of Southern Evangelical Seminary, has written several books on apologetics, and has spoken internationally.
Robert Velarde is a former atheist. He is the author of *Talking Sense with C.S. Lewis* and *The Lion, the Witch, and the Bible*. He is pursuing graduate studies in philosophy via Southern Evangelical Seminary.

"The greatest proof of Christianity for others is not how far a man can logically analyze his reasons for believing, but how far in practice he will stake his life on his belief."

—T.S. Eliot

Resources

The inclusion of a work does not necessarily mean endorsement of all its contents or of other works by the same author(s).

BOOKS

20 Compelling Evidences That God Exists by Kenneth D. Boa and Robert M. Bowman, Jr. (River Oak, 2002)

50 Proofs for the Bible: Old Testament (Rose Publishing, 2007)

50 Proofs for the Bible: New Testament (Rose Publishing, 2007)

Answering the Objections of Atheists, Agnostics, and Skeptics by Ron Rhodes (Harvest House, 2006)

Baker Encyclopedia of Christian Apologetics by Norman Geisler (Baker, 1999)

Christianity On Trial by Vincent Carroll and David Shiflett (Encounter Books, 2002)

Darwin on Trial by Phillip E. Johnson (InterVarsity, 1993)

Darwin's Black Box by Michael Behe (Free Press, 1998)

Does God Exist? by William Lane Craig, Stan W. Wallace, and Anthony Flew (Ashgate, 2003)

Does God Exist? by J.P. Moreland and Kai Nielsen (Thomas Nelson, 1990)

How Blind is the Watchmaker? by Neil Broom (InterVarsity, 2001)

God? A Debate Between a Christian and an Atheist by William Lane Craig and Walter Sinnott-Armstrong (Oxford University Press, 2004)

God's Universe by Owen Gingerich (Belknap Press, 2006)

Handbook of Christian Apologetics by Peter Kreeft and Ronald K. Tacelli (InterVarsity, 1994)

Icons of Evolution by Jonathan Wells (Regnery, 2000)

I Don't Have Enough Faith to be an Atheist by Norman Geisler and Frank Turek (Crossway, 2004)

Jesus Among Other Gods by Ravi Zacharias (Word, 2000)

Mere Christianity by C.S. Lewis (Macmillan, 1952).

More Than a Carpenter by Josh McDowell (Tyndale, 1977)

New Dictionary of Christian Apologetics edited by W.C. Campbell-Jack and Gavin McGrath (InterVarsity, 2006)

No Doubt About It by Winfried Corduan (Broadman & Holman, 1997)

Philosophical Foundations for a Christian Worldview by J.P. Moreland and William Lane Craig (InterVarsity, 2003)

Scaling the Secular City by J.P. Moreland (Baker, 1987)

Signs of Intelligence edited by William A. Dembski and James M. Kushiner (Brazos Press, 2001)

Stand: Core Truths You Must Know for an Unshakable Faith by Alex McFarland (Tyndale, 2005)

The 10 Most Common Objections to Christianity (And How to Effectively Answer Them) by Alex McFarland (Regal, 2007)

The Abolition of Man by C.S. Lewis (Macmillan, 1947)

The Case for a Creator by Lee Strobel (Zondervan, 2004)

The Case for Faith by Lee Strobel (Zondervan, 2000)

The Language of God: A Scientist Presents Evidence for Belief by Francis Collins (Free Press, 2006)

The Roots of Evil by Norman Geisler (Zondervan, 1978)

The Twilight of Atheism by Alister McGrath (Doubleday, 2004)

The Universe Next Door by James W. Sire (InterVarsity, 2004)

To Everyone An Answer edited by Francis J. Beckwith, William Lane Craig, and J.P. Moreland (InterVarsity, 2004)

When Critics Ask by Norman Geisler and Thomas Howe (Victor, 1992)

When Skeptics Ask by Norman Geisler and Ron Brooks (Victor, 1990)

Why I Am a Christian edited by Norman Geisler and Paul Hoffman (Baker, 2001)

Why Mike's Not a Christian by Ben Young (Harvest House, 2006)

Why Trust the Bible? (Rose Publishing, 2008)

Without a Doubt by Kenneth Richard Samples (Baker, 2004)

VIDEO/DVD

The Case for a Creator (Illustra Media, 2006)

The Privileged Planet (Illustra Media, 2004)

The Question of God: Sigmund Freud and C.S. Lewis (PBS, 2004)

Unlocking the Mystery of Life (Illustra Media, 2002)

POWERPOINT®

10 Questions and Answers on Atheism and Agnosticism (Rose Publishing, 2007)

100 Proofs for the Bible (Rose Publishing, 2007)

Evidence for the Resurrection (Rose Publishing, 2004)

Why Trust the Bible? (Rose Publishing, 2007)

INTERNET

Access Research Network   www.arn.org

Apologetics.com   www.apologetics.com

Discovery Institute   www.discovery.org/csc/

Leadership U   www.leaderu.com

Lee Strobel   www.leestrobel.com

Norman Geisler   www.normgeisler.com

PAMPHLETS

50 Proofs for the Bible: Old Testament (Rose Publishing, 2007)

50 Proofs for the Bible: New Testament (Rose Publishing, 2007)

Answers to Evolution (Rose Publishing, 2004)

Tough Questions about Christianity (Rose Publishing, 2009)

What Christianity Has Done for the World (Rose Publishing, 2007)

Worldviews Comparison (Rose Publishing, 2007)

Myths about Spirituality

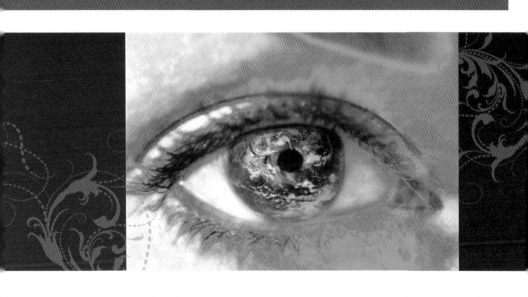

Myth: We are all "God."

Myth: Jesus is just one of many ways to the truth.

Myth: What I desire determines what happens to me.

Myth: I decide what is true for me.

What Makes Pop Spirituality So Popular?

YOU WILL BE AS GOD, whispered the serpent to Eve in the shadow of the Tree of the Knowledge of Good and Evil (Genesis 3:5)—the seductive suggestion that, instead of worshiping and serving God, we can possess divine power for ourselves. In the past few years, such claims have become increasingly fashionable on popular talk shows and in bestselling books.

+ Talk-show host Oprah Winfrey put it this way: "Jesus did not come to teach us how divine he was but to teach that divinity was within us."[1]

+ A book by Eckhart Tolle makes much the same point: "God," Tolle declares in *A New Earth*, "is ... the essence of who you are."[2]

+ "You are God in a physical body," claims *The Secret*, a book that topped the *New York Times* bestseller list. "You are Spirit in the flesh," the book goes on to say, "you are Eternal Life."[3]

Millions of people—many of whom also view themselves as followers of Jesus—have bought into the pop spirituality of celebrities like Oprah and Eckhart. Oprah Winfrey has been called "one of the most influential spiritual leaders in America.... To her audience of more than 22 million mostly female viewers, she has become ... an icon of church-free spirituality."[4] When Oprah announced a ten-week online seminar, engaging in a sentence-by-sentence study of Eckhart Tolle's spirituality, more than 700,000 people registered.

These popular forms of spirituality often use words, ideas, and even quotations from the Bible. Many people have assumed that the concepts are compatible with Christian faith. Yet, in truth, this spirituality has nothing to do with the actual beliefs of Jesus and his earliest followers. Proponents of pop spirituality may mention passages from the Bible, but they do not treat Scripture as an authoritative source for what we can know about God. In most cases, the words of Jesus and the apostles are exploited and misapplied as illustrations of me-centered spiritual themes. When compared with the overall message of Scripture, the central claims of pop spirituality directly contradict the good news of the gospel delivered through Jesus and his apostles (see Jude 1:3).

CONFLICTING BELIEFS

What are the specific ways that the concepts found in pop spirituality conflict with biblical truth? Although the teachings of today's spirituality differ from one another, there are five beliefs that the proponents of popular spirituality seem to share.

Myths of Today's Spirituality

+ Every human being is divine.

+ There are many paths to the truth about God.

+ The goal of my life is centered in me.

+ What I desire determines what happens in my life.

+ God's Word is not the final authority.

Can I be God?

WHAT DO POPULAR SPIRITUAL TEACHERS CLAIM?

You are God: "You are God in a physical body....You are a cosmic being. You are all power. You are all wisdom. You are all intelligence. You are perfection. You are magnificence. You are the creator, and you are creating the creation of You on this planet."[5] (Rhonda Byrne, *The Secret*)

You are a "cup of water" from the "ocean" of God: "I am so connected to the bigger picture of what God is, I realize I'm just a particle in the God-chain.... I see God as ocean, and I'm a cup of water from that ocean."[6] (Oprah Winfrey)

Divinity is within you: "Jesus did not come to teach us how divine he was but to teach that divinity was within us.... God isn't 'up there,' he exists in every one of us. It's up to us to seek the divine within."[7] (Oprah Winfrey paraphrasing Eric Butterworth, *Discover the Power Within You*)

There is no separation between you and God: "There can be no subject-object relationship here, no duality, no you and God.... Christ is your God-essence or Self, as it is sometimes called in the East.... Christ refers to your indwelling divinity regardless of whether you are conscious of it or not."[8] (Eckhart Tolle, *The Power of Now*)

You and God are One: "Until we know and realize that all of us are One, we cannot know and realize that we and God are One.... Stop seeing God as separate from you, and you as separate from each other."[9] (Neale Donald Walsch, *Conversations with God: An Uncommon Dialogue, Book 2*) "Your true nature...is one with the nature of God."[10] (Tolle, *A New Earth*)

WHAT DID THE FIRST FOLLOWERS OF JESUS TEACH?

God and humanity are distinct: God created human beings in his image, with the capacity to reflect God's nature by living in loving fellowship with other people and with God (see Gen. 1:26–28; 5:1–2; 9:6–7). Yet, the Bible makes a clear distinction between God and his creation: "In the beginning God created [*brought into existence from nothing*] the heavens and the earth.... God created man in his own image" (Gen. 1:1, 27; see also 2 Kings 19:15, 19; Isa. 43:7; 45:18).

No human being possesses "all power," "all wisdom," "all intelligence," or "perfection": Because every person has sinned and fallen short of God's glory (Rom. 3:23), no human being has all power, all wisdom, or all intelligence. God alone possesses perfect power and wisdom; God has revealed the fullness of his power, wisdom, and glory in Jesus Christ (Rom. 16:27; 1 Cor. 1:24; Eph. 1:17).

Jesus alone is God in human flesh: Jesus was and is uniquely divine (John 1:1, 14, 18; 20:28). No other human being can ever be divine in the same way as Jesus; Jesus was the "one and only" or "uniquely begotten" divine Son (John 3:16, 18).

No human being can ever become divine: According to Israel's central confession of faith, which Jesus himself affirmed, "The LORD our God, the LORD is one" (Deut. 6:4; Mark 12:29). In the New Testament, Paul stated that "there is one God" (1 Tim. 2:5). People may become "one" with God in the sense of sharing God's mission and purpose (see John 17:21). Yet the teaching of Scripture is clear: From the beginning of time (Gen. 1:26–28) to the end of time and beyond (Rev. 22:14–15), God and humanity remain distinct.

THE TRUTH: You are a wonderful creation of God, lovingly formed in God's image…but you cannot become God, and you do not possess perfect power or wisdom. You were created to worship, honor, glorify, and enjoy God for his perfect power and wisdom.

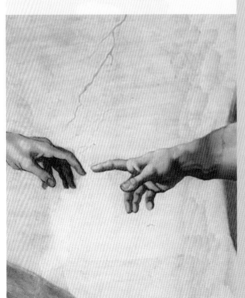

Where did the "secret" come from?

The cover of *The Secret* claims to contain a mystery that has been "passed down through the ages, highly coveted, hidden, lost, stolen, and bought for vast sums of money." In truth, this supposed secret is less than two centuries old, and it's not been "hidden, lost, stolen"—for the most part, it's simply been ignored because it's been recognized as a fraud.

The Secret and other similar books are based on ideas from the "New Thought Movement" that emerged in the nineteenth century. Phineas Parkhurst Quimby and other similar teachers believed that the human mind emitted unseen energies that could produce healing and prosperity. These ideas persisted into the early twentieth century. Wallace Wattles' *The Science of Getting Rich,* the book from which Rhonda Byrne borrowed "the law of attraction," was published in 1910.

How many ways are there to find the truth about God?

WHAT DO POPULAR SPIRITUAL TEACHERS CLAIM?

There are many paths to God; God does not care whether you believe in Jesus: "One of the biggest mistakes humans make is to believe that there is only one way. Actually there are many diverse paths leading to what you call God.... There could not possibly be only one way.... Does God care about your heart or whether you called His Son Jesus?"[11] (Oprah) "How 'spiritual' you are has nothing to do with what you believe.... All religions are equally false and equally true, depending on how you use them."[12] (Tolle, *A New Earth*)

If Jesus intended himself to be worshiped as God, Jesus was an egotist: "If what we are taught in orthodox religion when you go to church and you adore Jesus and praise Jesus [is true,] it means Jesus would have been the biggest egotist

that ever lived, if that was his purpose in coming to the world to have people adore him and worship him and carry on about him as people do.... Jesus did not come to teach us how divine he was but to teach that divinity was within us."[13] (Oprah)

The historical Jesus of the Gospels and the Jesus that Christians trust as Savior are fictional characters; the goal of the true Jesus is for you to achieve consciousness of your own divinity: "The first Jesus was a rabbi who wandered the shores of northern Galilee many centuries ago.... This historical Jesus has been lost, however, swept away by history.... (If you live in the East, his name might be Buddha, but the man is equally mythical and equally a projection of our own lack.)... Millions of people worship another Jesus, however, who never existed, who doesn't even lay claim to the fleeting substance of the first Jesus.... He is...the Three-in-One Christ, the source of sacraments and prayers that were unknown to the rabbi Jesus when he walked the earth.... These two versions of Jesus...hold a tragic aspect for me, because I blame them for stealing something precious: the Jesus who taught his followers how to reach God-consciousness.... Jesus spoke of the necessity to believe in him as the road to salvation, but those words were put into his mouth by followers writing decades later.... Finding God-consciousness through your own efforts happens in the present."[14] (Deepak Chopra, *The Third Jesus*)

WHAT DID THE FIRST FOLLOWERS OF JESUS TEACH?

Jesus is the only source of salvation: "Salvation is found in no one else, for there is no other name under heaven given to men by which we must be saved" (Acts 4:12). From this text, it is clear that God *does* care both about our hearts and about whether we believe explicitly in Jesus.

All religions are not the same: Every religion cannot be "equally false and equally true" because each religion makes claims that contradict the beliefs of other religions. Buddhism, for example, denies the existence of God while Hinduism recognizes many divine beings as expressions of one deity. Christian faith, however, states that truth and salvation are found only through Jesus Christ—a claim that is not found in any other religion. John emphasized the exclusiveness of this salvation with these words: "Whoever believes in the Son has eternal life, but whoever rejects the Son will not see life, for God's wrath remains on him" (John 3:36). The apostle Paul put it this way: "For there is one God and one mediator between God and men, the man Christ Jesus" (1 Tim. 2:5).

Jesus himself declared that he was God, and he allowed himself to be worshiped as God: In John 8:58, Jesus said, "I tell you the truth," Jesus answered, "before Abraham was born, I AM!"—a clear reference to Exodus 3:14, where God declared his holy name to be "I AM who I AM." Throughout the New Testament Gospels, Jesus allowed his disciples to worship him as God (see Matthew 14:33; 28:17; Luke 24:52; John 9:38; 20:28).

Jesus himself stated that he is the only pathway to God: Jesus said, "I am the way and the truth and the life. No one comes to the Father except through me" (John 14:6). According to Eckhart Tolle, this text implies that *every person* is "Truth": Tolle has claimed, "The Truth is inseparable from who you are.... Jesus tried to convey that when he said, 'I am the way and the truth and the life.'"[15] However, Tolle has misunderstood this text: *Jesus was speaking exclusively about himself; Jesus alone is life, truth, and the guide to God the Father.* Such claims do not make Jesus an "egotist," as Oprah Winfrey has claimed. Jesus made these claims because he truly was God in human flesh—something that no other person ever has been or will be.

The words of Jesus in the New Testament Gospels were not "put into his mouth" by later followers; these words come from eyewitnesses of his life, death, and resurrection: From the beginnings of Christian faith in the first century AD, believers in Jesus rejected testimony about Jesus that could not be connected to eyewitnesses of the risen Lord Jesus.[16] As such, there is every reason to trust that the words found in the New Testament Gospels accurately describe what Jesus did and truthfully report the essence of his message.

THE TRUTH: In Jesus Christ, God himself came to earth to reveal truth about himself. Only through Jesus Christ can anyone experience the truth and salvation that God offers.

Key Ideas in Pop Spirituality

Consciousness (also, "God-consciousness" or "Christ-consciousness"). Awareness of one's own divinity and of the oneness of all reality. Similar to the supposed insight and experiences that people known as "Gnostics" (AD 1–300) identified as *gnosis* or "knowledge."

Gnosticism (from Greek, *ginosko,* "I have knowledge"). Sect that emerged within or parallel to the Christian movement in the first and second centuries AD. Gnostics claimed to possess secret knowledge about God that was unavailable to others. Gnostics viewed the physical world and its Creator—usually identified with the God of the Old Testament—as evil. According to Gnostics, Jesus Christ was not God in human flesh. He was a divine spirit in what appeared to be a human body; his mission was to free people from the limitations of the physical world.

Monism (from Greek *monos* [oneness]). Belief that any apparent distinctions among people or between people and God are an illusion; all is one. Buddhism is an essentially monistic religion. By describing God as "holy" and "almighty"—that is to say, *separate from* and *sovereign over* creation—the Scriptures reject monism (see Gen. 17:1; Rev. 4:8).

Pantheism (from Greek *pan* [all] + *theos* [deity]). Belief that all is divine, that God and the living universe are indistinguishable. Hinduism is a pantheistic religion. Genesis 1:1 rules out pantheism by affirming that God brought the universe into existence from nothing. If God *is* the universe, God could not *create* the universe.

Spirituality What persons believe about and how they respond to the transcendent or spiritual aspects of their existence.

What is the goal of my life?

WHAT DO POPULAR SPIRITUAL TEACHERS CLAIM?

Your purpose is to be happy: "Be happy now. Feel good now. That's the only thing you have to do.... 'If it ain't fun, don't do it.'"[17] (Byrne, *The Secret*)

You determine your own purpose in life: "Your purpose is what you say it is. Your mission is the mission you give yourself.... The earth turns on its orbit for You. The oceans ebb and flow for You. The birds sing for You. The sun rises and it sets for You. The stars come out for You. Every beautiful thing you see, every wondrous thing you experience, is all there for You. Take a look around. None of it can exist without You. No matter who you thought you were, now you know the Truth of Who You Really Are."[18] (Byrne, *The Secret*)

The ultimate goal for your life is the evolution of your consciousness of yourself as God: "Jesus ... taught his followers how to reach God-consciousness."[19] (Chopra) "Life will give you whatever experience is most helpful for the evolution of your consciousness."[20] (Tolle, *A New Earth*)

WHAT DID THE FIRST FOLLOWERS OF JESUS TEACH?

Before the world began, God designed each person for a specific and glorious purpose: For believers in Jesus Christ, the goal and purpose of life is to reflect God's glory through lives that conform increasingly to the character of Jesus. The apostle Paul put it this way in a letter to one early church: "For we are God's workmanship, created in Christ Jesus to do good works, which God prepared in advance for us to do" (Eph. 2:10). Paul wrote to another church, "Each of you should look not only to your own interests, but also to the interests of others. Your attitude should be the same as that of Christ Jesus" (Phil. 2:4–5).

The growth for which God created humanity is growth in the knowledge of Jesus Christ—not "evolution" in one's own consciousness: "Grow in the grace and knowledge of our Lord and Savior Jesus Christ" (2 Peter 3:18; see also 2 Cor. 10:15; Eph. 4:15–16; Col. 1:10).

God calls people to turn from their own purposes and to embrace his purpose for their lives: Jesus began his earthly ministry with these words: "Repent [*turn from your present direction in life*] and believe the good news! " (Mark 1:15). Later, Jesus informed those who wanted to follow him, "If anyone would come after me, he must deny himself and take up his cross and follow me. For whoever wants to save his life will lose it, but whoever loses his life for me and for the gospel will save it" (Mark 8:34–35).

THE TRUTH: God designed you to grow in his grace and to reflect his glory. He has already determined a purpose for your life—and the purpose that he has designed for you is far greater than any purpose that you might form on your own.

Does what I desire determine what happens to me?

WHAT DO POPULAR SPIRITUAL TEACHERS CLAIM?

By concentrating your attention on certain desires for prolonged periods of time, you can gain anything you want; this is "the Secret" or "the law of attraction": "Just like the law of gravity, the law of attraction never slips up.... There are no exclusions to the law of attraction.... The Secret gives you anything you want: happiness, health, and wealth. You can have, do, or be anything you want.... Like attracts like.... Thoughts become things. It is exactly like placing an order from a catalogue.... You must know that what you want is yours the moment you ask.... See yourself living in abundance and you will attract it. It works every time, with every person."[21] (Byrne, *The Secret*)

If tragedy or poverty plagues your life, it is because you attracted misfortune through your own imperfect thinking: "If something came to you, you drew it, with prolonged thought.... Imperfect thoughts are the cause of all humanity's ills, including disease, poverty, and unhappiness.... Thoughts are magnetic, and thoughts have a

frequency. As you think, those thoughts are sent out into the universe and they magnetically attract all like things that are on the same frequency."[22] (Byrne, *The Secret*)

Biblical characters became wealthy by using the law of attraction: "Abraham, Isaac, Jacob, Joseph, Moses, and Jesus were not only prosperity teachers but also millionaires themselves, with more affluent lifestyles than many present-day millionaires could conceive of."[23] (Byrne, *The Secret*)

WHAT DID THE FIRST FOLLOWERS OF JESUS TEACH?

Your thoughts are not the ultimate cause of the events in your life. Thoughts *are* important; Paul even calls the people of God to "take every thought to make it obedient to Christ" (2 Cor. 10:5). Your thoughts do not, however, determine the events in your life. Some events in this world occur because of people's choices (see, for example, Prov. 24:30–34). All events occur because God directly causes them or because God allows them to happen (Job 1:7–12; 2:1–7). Many happen for reasons that are unexplainable at the time (Ecc. 2:20–26; 7:14–15). In every case, God is, however, ultimately in control: "I am the LORD, and there is no other," God declared through the prophet Isaiah. "I form the light and create darkness, I bring prosperity and create disaster; I, the LORD, do all these things" (Isa. 45:6–7). God is working in every circumstance for the good of those who love him (Rom. 8:28). Under no circumstances do well-being and misfortune come into people's lives merely because their thoughts have "magnetically" attracted these situations.

Misfortune does not occur because of your "imperfect thoughts" but because you live in an imperfect world: Because the first human beings chose to rebel against God, not only sin but also misfortune and death entered into the world. "Sin came into the world through one man," the apostle Paul wrote, "and death through sin" (Rom. 5:12). This death affected every part of life: "Creation was subjected to frustration ... in hope that the creation itself will be liberated from its bondage to decay," Paul continued. "The whole creation has been groaning as in the pains of childbirth right up to the present time" (Rom. 8:20–22).

Biblical heroes were not "prosperity teachers," and the wealth that they possessed was not achieved through a "law of attraction": While Abraham, Isaac, Jacob, Joseph, and Moses may have possessed some wealth, there is no evidence that they gained prosperity through a secret "law of attraction." These characters inherited, worked, and—in the case of Jacob—schemed to accumulate what they possessed. As for Jesus, the claim of *The Secret* is absolutely false. Jesus was no "prosperity teacher," and he certainly was not a millionaire. Jesus did not even have a home: "Foxes have holes and birds of the air have nests," he told one inquirer, "but the Son of Man has no place to lay his head" (Matt. 8:20; Luke 9:58). When he died, he was even buried in a borrowed tomb (John 19:38–42).

THE TRUTH: Your thoughts and attitudes are important, but your "prolonged thought" does not determine the events or circumstances of your life. Some circumstances occur because of poor choices, others occur for reasons that are humanly unexplainable, and others are the direct result of God's choice to act in human history—but no event occurs outside the control of God.

take every
thought
to make it
obedient
to Christ

Who determines what is true?

WHAT DO POPULAR SPIRITUAL TEACHERS CLAIM?

You are the truth: "The Truth is inseparable from who you are. Yes, you *are* the Truth. If you look for it elsewhere, you will be deceived every time."[24] (Tolle, *A New Earth*)

The answers you need are found in popular spiritual teachers: "If you are seeking an answer or guidance on something in your life, ask the question, believe you will receive, and then open this book [*The Secret*] randomly. At the exact place where the pages fall open will be the guidance and answer you are seeking."[25] (Byrne, *The Secret*)

You determine what is right and wrong: "Whatever you choose for You is right."[26] (Byrne, *The Secret*)

WHAT DID THE FIRST FOLLOWERS OF JESUS TEACH?

You are not the truth; God is truth: According to the prophet Isaiah, God is the "God of truth" (Isa. 65:16), and he has revealed his "grace and truth ... through Jesus Christ" (John 1:17). Jesus himself declared, "I am the way and the truth and the life" (John 14:6; see also John 18:37).

By telling the truth about God's will and God's actions in human history, the Scriptures provide the guidance and answers that you need: According to Jesus, "Scripture"—which, at the time of his earthly ministry, referred to the Old Testament—represented the authoritative record of God's dealings with humanity. "Scripture cannot be broken," Jesus said (John 10:35), and he proclaimed the Scriptures as absolute truth (Luke 24:25–27). His first followers treated Scripture in the same way (Acts 1:16; 8:35; 17:2). Even in the first century AD, Christians recognized not only the Old Testament but also the written testimony of eyewitnesses of the resurrected Lord Jesus as "Scripture" (2 Peter 3:16). In a letter written near the end of Paul's life, Paul summarized the early church's perspective on Scripture: "The holy Scriptures ... are able to make you wise for salvation through faith in Christ Jesus. All Scripture is God-breathed and is useful for teaching, rebuking, correcting and training in righteousness" (2 Tim. 3:15–17). The authority that stands behind the Scriptures is the authority of God himself.

God is the ultimate standard for what is right and wrong: God alone is righteous (Mark 10:18; Rev. 15:4), whereas the human heart is "deceitful above all things and desperately wicked" (Jer. 17:9). Only God can provide a perfect standard for what is true and good.

THE TRUTH: God is the truth, and his truth has been revealed through Jesus Christ. By telling the truth about God's will and God's actions throughout human history, the Bible provides the guidance and answers that you need.

© MBPHOTO

Why is pop spirituality so attractive?

Human beings come equipped with a spiritual longing, a thirst for something beyond themselves. Popular talk shows and books offer attractive formulas for spiritual fulfillment:

"You are God in a physical body." (Byrne, *The Secret*)

"I see God as ocean, and I'm a cup of water from that ocean." (Oprah)

All religions are equally false and equally true, depending on how you use them." (Tolle, *A New Earth*)

"Jesus … taught his followers how to reach God-consciousness." (Chopra)

"Thoughts are magnetic, and thoughts have a frequency. As you think, those thoughts are sent out into the universe and they magnetically attract all like things that are on the same frequency." (Byrne, *The Secret*)

Pop spirituality seems to offer a relief for people's anxieties, fears, desires, and dreams. It provides apparent control over the chaos of life, a formula for success and improvement.

In reality, we long for the relationship with God for which we were created.

What is the real secret everyone is looking for?

In every human heart, God has placed a longing for wisdom and knowledge that seems hidden. "He has," in the words of one sage, "set eternity in the heart, yet no one can discover the full work that God has done from beginning to end" (Ecc. 3:11). Ultimately, this longing is intended to guide humanity toward God himself. God is both the secret and the answer for which your soul is seeking, and he has revealed his identity in Jesus Christ "in whom are hidden all the treasures of wisdom and knowledge" (Col. 2:3).

How Teachers of Popular Spirituality misuse the Bible

Teachers such as Eckhart Tolle often quote Bible verses in books and seminars, leading many people to assume that what these teachers say is compatible with Christian faith.

The problem is, these teachers of pop spirituality regularly misunderstand and misapply the texts that they quote. (See the chart on the following pages.)

HOW CAN YOU LEARN TO RECOGNIZE WHEN POPULAR TEACHERS ARE MISUSING BIBLICAL TEXTS?

1. Carefully read the entire context of the verse.

2. Study the historical background of the text, to see how people understood the text when it was written.

3. Learn more about the text from a reliable study tool such as:
   + *New Bible Commentary* (InterVarsity Press)
   + *The IVP Bible Background Commentary* (InterVarsity Press)
   + *The NIV Application Commentary* (Zondervan)

4. Pray to the Holy Spirit for guidance and wisdom.

Such misuse of the Scriptures is not new. In the second century AD, a group known as Gnostics twisted many biblical texts to fit their own beliefs. Irenaeus, a prominent second-century pastor, described their practices in this way:

"They gather their views from sources other than the Scriptures, but then they rework ... the Lord's parables, the prophets' sayings, and the apostles' words to fit their own peculiar assertions, disregarding the orderliness and connections in the Scriptures.... It is as if they disassemble the individual jewels from an artist's depiction of a king, then rearrange those jewels to look like a dog or perhaps a fox."[32]

Examples of misused Scripture:

WHAT DOES THE TEXT SAY?	"Be perfect, therefore, as your heavenly Father is perfect" (Matt. 5:48).	"If anyone would come after me, he must deny himself and take up his cross and follow me" (Mark 8:34).
WHAT DID THE TEXT MEAN IN ITS CONTEXT?	Live every part of your life according to God's perfect standard, not according to the imperfect standards of human tradition.	Following Jesus is costly. To follow Jesus, you must give up control of everything to God, even to the point of death.
HOW DO TEACHERS OF POP SPIRITUALITY MISREPRESENT THIS TEXT?	**Tolle:** "'Be ye whole, even as your Father in Heaven is whole.' The New Testament's 'Be ye perfect' is a mistranslation of the original Greek word, which means whole. That is to say, you don't need to become whole, but *be* what you already are."[27]	**Tolle:** "What I perceive, experience, think, or feel is not ultimately who I am.... The Buddha was probably the first human being to see this clearly, and so *anata* (no self) became one of the central points of his teaching. And when Jesus said, 'Deny thyself,' what he meant was: Negate—and thus undo—the illusion of self."[28]
WHAT'S THE PROBLEM?	Although the Greek word in this text *can* mean "whole," in the Bible "wholeness" and "perfection" mean conformity to God's ways. Tolle misunderstands the biblical concept of wholeness and claims that it means being what you already are—the opposite of its literary and historical meaning.	Immediately after Jesus' statement, it is clear that he intends his followers to preserve their "souls" *not* by denying the *existence* of self but by giving themselves completely to Jesus (Mark 8:35–37). Tolle's interpretation forces Buddhist concepts from another time and another culture into the words of Jesus.

"Therefore I tell you, whatever you ask for in prayer, believe that you have received it, and it will be yours" (Mark 11:24).	"I am the way and the truth and the life. No one comes to the Father except through me" (John 14:6).	"I saw a new heaven and a new earth, for the first heaven and the first earth had passed away" (Rev. 21:1).
This teaching of Jesus begins with the words, "Have faith in God" or "Trust God" (Mark 11:22)—which includes surrendering your will to God's will. What this means is that God can and will do anything we request in conformity to his will.	Jesus was informing his followers that the only way to live in fellowship with his Father was by following Jesus as the only source of truth and life.	At the end of time, God will create heaven and earth anew, wiping away the fallenness of this present world.
Byrne: "Ask. Make a command to the universe. Let the universe know what you want. The universe responds to your thoughts.... Believe in the unseen.... The final step in the process is to receive.... In this process it's important to feel good, to be happy, because when you're feeling good you're putting yourself in the frequency of what you want."[29]	**Tolle:** "The very Being that you are is Truth. Jesus tried to convey that when he said, 'I am the way and the truth and the life.' These words uttered by Jesus are one of the most powerful and direct pointers to the Truth. If misinterpreted, however, they become a great obstacle. Jesus speaks of the innermost 'I Am,' the essence identity of every man and woman, every life-form, in fact."[30]	**Tolle:** "Heaven ... refers to the inner realm of consciousness. This is the esoteric meaning of the word, and this is also its meaning in the teachings of Jesus. 'A new heaven' is the emergence of a transformed state of human consciousness, and 'a new earth' is its reflection in the physical realm."[31]
The contributors to *The Secret* misunderstand this biblical text as a tool to receive whatever the reader wants. But Jesus' words are focused on trusting God so deeply that you desire his will to be done above any of your own desires.	Throughout John's Gospel, it's clear that Jesus is the unique incarnation (embodiment) of God, the true "I am." (John 1:1, 14, 18; 8:58; 20:28). In John 14:6, Jesus was *not* referring to a mystic "essence identity of every man and woman." Jesus was describing himself as the only pathway to fellowship with the heavenly Father.	In the biblical text, the word "heaven" is the same as the word for "skies." Throughout Scripture, "heaven" or "skies" consistently points to the realm that is beyond humanity—not to some "inner realm of consciousness." Tolle's "esoteric meaning" contradicts the meaning of "heaven" that appears throughout the Bible.

RESOURCES FOR FURTHER STUDY

Garlow, James and Marschall, Rick. *The Secret Revealed: Exposing the Truth About the Law of Attraction*. FaithWords, 2007

Jones, Peter. *The Gnostic Empire Strikes Back: An Old Heresy for the New Age,* P & R Publishing, 1992.

Jones, Timothy Paul. *Conspiracies and the Cross*, Frontline, 2008.

Pamphlets from Rose Publishing:

26 Ways to Explain the Gospel (Rose Publishing, 2009).

Creeds and Heresies: Then & Now (Rose Publishing, 2009).

Essential Doctrine Made Easy by Norman L. Geisler (Rose Publishing, 2007).

How to Study the Bible (Rose Publishing, 2007).

Notes

1 The Oprah Winfrey Show, video on file with The Watchman Fellowship.

2 E. Tolle, *A New Earth* (New York; Penguin, 2005) 184.

3 R. Byrne, *The Secret* (New York: Atria, 2006) 164.

4 L. Taylor, "The Church of O," *Christianity Today* (April 1, 2002): http://www.christianitytoday.com.

5 R. Byrne, *The Secret*, 164.

6 B. Adler, ed., *The Uncommon Wisdom of Oprah* (New York: Citadel, 1997, 2000) 233.

7 The Oprah Winfrey Show, video on file with The Watchman Fellowship.

8 E. Tolle, *The Power of Now* (Novato, CA: New World, 1999, 2004) 224.

9 N.D. Walsch, *Conversations with God, Part 2* (Charlottesville, VA: Hampton Roads, 1997) 173.

10 E. Tolle, *A New Earth*, 184.

11 The Oprah Winfrey Show, retrieved September 2008, http://www.youtube.com/watch?v=ETeI6i5oqh4.

12 E. Tolle, *A New Earth*, 18, 70.

13 The Oprah Winfrey Show, video on file with The Watchman Fellowship.

14 D. Lemon, Interview with Deepak Chopra: http://transcripts.cnn.com/TRANSCRIPTS/0802/22/cnr.04.html; D. Chopra, *The Third Jesus,* chapter 1.

15 E. Tolle, *A New Earth*, 71.

16 For defenses of the essential historical accuracy of the New Testament Gospels, see T. Jones, *Misquoting Truth* (Downers Grove, IL: InterVarsity, 2007), and, T. Jones, *Conspiracies and the Cross* (Lake Mary, FL: FrontLine, 2008).

17 R. Byrne, *The Secret*, 179.

18 R. Byrne, *The Secret*, 183.

19 Selections from D. Chopra, *The Third Jesus* (New York: Harmony, 2008) 2–34.

20 E. Tolle, *A New Earth*, 41.

21 Selections from R. Byrne, *The Secret*, 27–36.

22 Selections from R. Byrne, *The Secret*, 7–25.

23 R. Byrne, *The Secret*, 109.

24 E. Tolle, *A New Earth*, 71.

25 R. Byrne, *The Secret*, 171–172.

26 R. Byrne, *The Secret*, 179.

27 E. Tolle, *A New Earth*, 184.

28 E. Tolle, *A New Earth*, 79.

29 Selections from R. Byrne, *The Secret*, 47–62.

30 E. Tolle, *A New Earth*, 71.

31 E. Tolle, *A New Earth*, 23.

32 Irenaeus of Lyons, *Adversus Haereses,* 1:8:1.

Author: Timothy Paul Jones, EdD is the bestselling author of *The Da Vinci Codebreaker* and *Conspiracies and the Cross*.

Myths about Angels

Myth: We should look to angels for guidance.

Myth: We become angels when we die.

Myth: We should expect angels to visit us.

Myth: All angels are wonderful and kind.

ANGELS: *Why the Fascination?*

It seems as though angels are everywhere! They're in bestselling books, top-rated TV shows, blockbuster movies, and even documentaries. The captivating, winged beings we see in stores and on the screen seem magical and clever, warm and whimsical, always willing to put up with human mistakes and help solve problems. They rescue people from crises and occasionally warn us to do what's right.

Hungry Hearts

It's a fact: The human heart longs for a gentle touch from a supernatural being—for forgiveness, guidance, and understanding. Many cultures have a long tradition of stories that feature noble genies, fairies, and gods. This yearning to have someone or something powerful on our side points to a truth made powerfully clear in the Bible: More exists than we can fully grasp with our five senses.

The Inside Story

This following pages will guide you through much of what Scripture discloses about angels—their origins, activities, and sometimes terrifying might. These amazing teachings are no secret; they've been in God's Word for thousands of years, and they're our sole reliable source about who angels really are and what they do.

The Other Side

While it's fun to think of angels as all warmth and light, the Bible warns us that many angels are evil, and they've deliberately chosen to reject God and goodness. What makes them especially dangerous is their use of appealing disguises to mislead people. The following pages reveal the differences between good angels and fallen angels—and underscore the reality that God's love and power are stronger than any angel could ever be.

Are not all angels ministering spirits sent to serve those who will inherit salvation?
HEBREWS 1:14

Praise the Lord, you his angels, you mighty ones who do his bidding, who obey his word.
PSALM 103:20

There is rejoicing in the presence of the angels of God over one sinner who repents.
LUKE 15:10

When God brings his firstborn [Jesus] into the world, he says, "Let all God's angels worship him."
HEBREWS 1:6

Should we look to angels for spiritual guidance?

Many people say...

Angels have lots to tell us about God and life. Angel enthusiasts today claim that we should look to angels to tell us about themselves, about God, heaven, and how we should live. Books have been published with titles like *Ask Your Angels, Messages from Your Angels,* and *Answers from the Angels.* Those who look to angels for guidance sometimes call them "spirit guides."

Sylvia Browne, a popular New Age psychic, claims that her spirit guide, named Francine, has told her all sorts of things about religion, including that Jesus didn't rise from the dead because he didn't actually die on the cross.[1]

© Arman Zhenikeyev

The Bible says...

Angels don't ordinarily communicate with human beings. In fact, no one in the Bible ever pursues communication with angels, or recommends seeking to hear from angels. When an angel appears to people in the Bible, it always comes as a total surprise to them. The most common opening words of an angel to a human are "Fear not" or "Do not be afraid" (Genesis 21:17; Matthew 28:5; Luke 1:13, 30; 2:10).

Unfortunately, not all angels or spiritual beings are on God's side. There are uncounted evil spirits— demons—who are the Devil's fallen angels (Matthew 25:41). You can't believe everything you hear from angelic beings any more than you can believe everything you hear from other people. Nor does the devil wear a bright red lapel pin with the name "Satan." He disguises himself as an angel of light (2 Corinthians 11:14).

Scripture is the means by which God conveys his truth to all of his people, the standard by which we should test all religious claims (Matthew 22:29; Acts 17:11; 2 Timothy 3:16). When God's angels speak to human beings, they don't contradict the Bible. The apostle Paul warns Christians not to accept another gospel, even if it seems to come from an angel in heaven (Galatians 1:6–9).

You should also know....

Seeking communication from angels risks opening a door to demonic influence. Since God's angels generally don't respond to efforts to initiate conversations with them, if any spiritual entity does reply, it's likely not to be from God. Receiving messages from spirits may sound exciting, but it's deceptive, since such "voices" aren't what they claim to be.

Some angel communication methods overtly involve the occult. New Age author

Doreen Virtue has created "The Angel Guidance Board" with dice and "angel markers" to help you receive messages from angels, including answers to your questions.[2] Using objects this way is exactly what occult practices are: Employing physical devices a in rituals to obtain hidden information or alter reality through supernatural means, especially by communication with spirits. God strongly rejects and forbids such practices (Deuteronomy 18:10–12).

2. Do angels have bodies?

Many people say...

Angels are physical beings. A lot of people today think that angels have physical bodies and look similar to humans. Others describe them not only as physical in appearance, but often overtly male or female. One author describes a particular angel as having "the face and form of a beautiful woman wearing a flowing white robe trimmed in gold."[3] Another author tells about a woman who saw an angel that "looked like a clean-cut, boy-next-door football player ... only larger and very muscular."[4] "Apostolic-prophetic" minister Steven Brooks claims, "Just as the human race includes male and female, so does the angelic race include male and female."[5]

The Bible says...

Angels are spirits—that is, they're beings who don't have bodies. Hebrews 1:7 (quoting Psalm 104:4) compares angels to wind and fire—bodiless, non-solid forces. Even more tellingly, the capacity of demonic spirits to inhabit the bodies of humans (Matthew 12:43–45; Luke 11:24–26) is evidence that spirits don't have bodies of their own.

The Bible gives no support to the idea that angels literally have male and female forms. The fact that Scripture never describes angels as female or feminine suggests that the masculine language used of angels is actually generic (or genderless). In fact, the Bible rarely gives any description of angels other than their typical appearance in bright light.

> "Praise him, all his angels, praise him, all his heavenly hosts. Praise him, sun and moon, praise him, all you shining stars. Praise him, you highest heavens and you waters above the skies. Let them praise the name of the LORD, for he commanded and they were created." PSALM 148:2–5

You should also know....

The Bible does report that angels visited Abraham and Lot and ate food with them (Genesis 18:8; 19:1–3). Some ancient Jewish interpreters, such as Philo of Alexandria and Josephus, thought that the angels only seemed to eat the food.[6]

Modern interpreters usually conclude that angels are capable of taking on a bodily form temporarily, during which time they can really eat food. Both explanations are consistent with the historic Jewish and Christian belief that angels are beings without bodies.

Will we become angels?

Many people say...

Angels are people who have died and gone to heaven. This belief (at least in its modern form) appears to have come from the teachings of 18th-century mystic Emanuel Swedenborg. According to Swedenborg, "there is not a single angel who was created as such at the beginning," but rather, all angels come from the human race; "we were created to become angels."[7]

This idea was evidently picked up by Joseph Smith, founder of the Mormon Church. Mormon doctrine teaches that "Angels ... are resurrected personages, having bodies of flesh and bones."[8] For example, Smith described a prophet named Moroni in the *Book of Mormon*, and claimed that Moroni had been transformed into an angel after death and appeared to him in a series of visitations.[9] Today, most Mormon temples feature a spire topped by a golden statue of the angel Moroni.

The Bible says...

Resurrected Christians will be "*like* the angels," but they won't *be* angels. According to Jesus, when Christians are raised from the dead they will resemble angels in two ways: First, they will be immortal beings, and second, they won't be getting married (Luke 20:34–36).

The Old Testament indicates that God created the angels around the same time that he made the physical universe, sometimes referring to them as "sons of God." The Lord asked Job, "Where were you when I laid the earth's foundation? Tell me, if you understand. Who marked off its dimensions? ... Who stretched a measuring line across it? On what were its footings set, or who laid its cornerstone—while the morning stars sang together and all the angels [literally, "sons of God"] shouted for joy?" (Job 38:4–7). Though the Bible doesn't reveal exactly when God made the angels, it's clear that he made them at a time before Job and all other human beings existed. Because God made the angels before he made humans, this shows that angels are not resurrected human beings— they're a different kind of being.

You should also know....

Believers in Jesus Christ go through two "stages" after they die:

- **First, their souls or spirits go to be with Christ** (2 Corinthians 5:1–5; Philippians 1:21–23).

- **Second, at Christ's second coming he will raise them from the dead as** glorified humans, with bodies like his (Romans 8:11; Philippians 3:21).

After his resurrection, Christ could eat and drink and be touched (Luke 24:36–43; John 20:16–29; Acts 10:40–41)—and we'll be like that, too. Also like Christ, we will be immortal, sinless beings (1 Corinthians 15:42–54).

Q: Do we each have a guardian angel?

Many people say...

Angels are assigned as bodyguards for every child. In popular folklore in many religions, including Christianity, guardian angels are thought to be assigned to each child at birth. According to the *Catholic Encyclopedia*, "That every individual soul has a guardian angel has never been defined by the Church, and is, consequently, not an article of faith; but it is the 'mind of the Church,' as St. Jerome expressed it: 'how great the dignity of the soul, since each one has from his birth an angel commissioned to guard it.'"[10]

More generally, some people are convinced that God promises that angels will protect those who believe. Some quote Psalm 91:11–12: "For he will command his angels concerning you to guard you in all your ways; they will lift you up in their hands, so that you will not strike your foot against a stone." Others cite Hebrews 1:14: "Are not all angels ministering spirits sent to serve those who will inherit salvation?"

The Bible says...

There's no real basis for believing in "guardian angels." Some people think that Jesus referred to guardian angels when he spoke about "little ones" (children) and "their angels in heaven" in Matthew 18:10. However, looking at Jesus' words in context, he isn't assuring people that children will never come to harm; instead, he's warning adults never to be the cause of children "stumbling" or sinning (verses 3–6). "See that you do not look down on one of these little ones. For I tell you that their angels in heaven always see the face of my Father in heaven" (verse 10). Note that these angels aren't watching the children, but looking to God— probably awaiting orders from God to avenge anyone who despises or abuses children.

Luke's account of an angel helping Peter escape from jail (Acts 12:6–15) doesn't support the idea that Peter had a guardian angel even though the passage reports that some of his friends mistakenly believed the servant girl had seen "his angel" (verse 15). The passage states that the Lord *sent* the angel for that occasion and that the angel *left* after Peter's escape (verses 10–11). Clearly, then, this was not a guardian angel.

You should also know....

Psalm 91:11–12 should probably be understood as a prophetic picture of the Messiah, who had a perfect relationship with God. God protected his Messiah, Jesus, from all harm through his angels— until Jesus willingly laid down his life for our salvation.

The way that angels "serve" Christians in the context of Hebrews 1:14 is by bringing messages from God of importance to our salvation (Hebrews 2:2–3). And despite what some people claim, no biblical text gives any indication that angels assist us with our money or business, or help us work out our family problems. Rather, the Bible tells us to look to God for guidance and help in all our daily concerns: "Do not be anxious about anything, but in everything, by prayer and petition, with thanksgiving, present your requests to God. And the peace of God, which transcends all understanding, will guard your hearts and your minds in Christ Jesus" (Philippians 4:6–7).

5   Should we expect angels to visit us?

Many people say...

Angels are appearing to people all the time. According to New Age writer Doreen Virtue, "*those who are willing and ready to see angels will see angels.*"[11] Popular author Karen Goldman asserts, "Angels are speaking to everyone. Some of us are only listening better."[12] Evangelists Charles and Frances Hunter write, "We could fill columns relating the wonderful things God has done for us through His ministering angels. We could write story after story ... about angelic visitations to us."[13]

Hebrews 13:2, which says "Be not forgetful to entertain strangers: for thereby some have entertained angels unawares" (KJV), has been taken to imply that "we've probably *all* seen angels at some time in our lives—without knowing it."[14]

The Bible says...

Angel appearances are usually important and generally uncommon. Although the Bible reports appearances of angels to human beings, a careful review of these accounts indicates that such events—even in biblical times—were rare, exceptional experiences, and presumably are at least as rare today.

Angels appeared to people to announce the miraculous births of key figures (Isaac, John the Baptist, and of course Jesus), to call prophets and other leaders to ministry (Isaiah), to bring divine revelations (Ezekiel, John), to deliver or strengthen prophets (Elijah, Elisha, Daniel) and apostles (Peter, Paul), to announce Jesus' resurrection to the women at the tomb, and on other significant occasions. Most of these individuals saw angels only once in their lifetimes. The Bible does not teach or suggest that we should expect angels to visit or appear to people for more ordinary reasons.

The main point of Hebrews 13:2 is that we should show hospitality to strangers, not that we might normally encounter angels. The verse probably refers to the hospitality that Lot showed to visitors who did turn out to be angels (Genesis 19). Indeed, one never knows who strangers will turn out to be, but their being angels is highly unlikely.

Most important of all, Christians should resist the temptation of focusing their energy and hopes on meeting angels when they can have a rich, personal relationship with the very *Maker* of the angels (1 Peter 1:8–12; see Question 9).

You should also know....

The idea that persons with a special faith in the ministry of angels are more likely to see angels has no biblical support whatsoever. In most of the biblical appearances of angels, the people who see them are totally taken by surprise. In not one account in the Bible does anyone seek an encounter with an angel. No one ever prays to see an angel or expresses any expectation of seeing one.

6. Aren't all angels wonderful and kind?

Many people say...

We can count on angels to be good and helpful. Many people in the occult and New Age encourage us to believe that all angels are here to help us.

Modern-day witch Silver Ravenwolf denies that fallen or evil angels exist, and writes that "angels create bridges between various religions" and "will assist you in connecting with your higher self."[15]

Some believe that even if there are bad angels, one need not fear them. Doreen Virtue advises that the "average person, living and praying with good intentions, doesn't have to worry about fallen angels." Such angels are actually "negative thought-forms" that cannot disguise themselves as good angels.[16]

You should also know....

While Christians should be on their guard against Satan (1 Peter 5:8), they are not to fear him or the demons (2 Thessalonians 3:3; 1 John 4:4). Instead of focusing on Satan, Christians need to submit to God and the Devil will flee from them (James 4:7).

The Bible says...

There are *two* kinds of angels: good ones and evil ones. In fact, Satan—whose name means "adversary" and whom the Bible portrays as God's chief enemy—is an angel. Jesus refers to Satan as a real being (Matthew 12:26; 13:39; Mark 4:15; Luke 10:18; John 8:44).

According to Revelation 12:9 other angels rebelled with Satan when he was cast down to Earth: "The great dragon was hurled down— that ancient serpent called the devil, or Satan, who leads the whole world astray. He was hurled to the earth, and his angels with him." These are fallen angels, also called "evil spirits," "unclean spirits," or "demons," in contrast to the "holy angels" who serve God (Matthew 25:31; Luke 9:26; Acts 10:22; Revelation 14:10).

The Gospels describe fallen angels as possessing people or causing illness, and numerous passages describe Jesus demonstrating his authority over them by commanding and casting them out (for example, Matthew 8:28–32).

The New Testament warns that fallen angels are actively involved in opposing Christians through deception and false teaching: "In later times some will abandon the faith and follow deceiving spirits and things taught by demons" (1 Timothy 4:1).

The Bible teaches that at the final judgment, Satan and the demons will be cast into the lake of fire "prepared for the devil and his angels" (Revelation 20:10; Matthew 25:41). Their destination is also called the "abyss," or bottomless pit (Revelation 9:2, 11; 11:7; 17:8; 20:3).

7. Do angels start new religions?

Many people say...

God sent an angel to start a religion that replaces historic Christianity. Some religions claim that they were started when God sent an angel with a message that resulted in a new scripture supplementing or correcting the Bible.

Islam claims that God revealed himself to Muhammad by sending the angel Gabriel with the message that Muhammad should "recite" what God prompted him to say. The result was the series of speeches collected after Muhammad's death into a book called the *Qur'an* (*Koran*), which Muslims believe takes the place of the Bible.[17]

Joseph Smith, the founder of Mormonism, declared that an angel named Moroni led him to a spot on a hill in upstate New York where golden plates containing a lost ancient scripture were buried. Smith also claimed that God inspired him to translate those plates from an unknown form of Egyptian into English. Smith published the work, entitled the *Book of Mormon*, in 1830, the same year he organized what's now known as the Church of Jesus Christ of Latter-day Saints.[18]

The Bible says...

We must compare any new religion or any new form of Christianity with the teachings of the apostles in the New Testament, even if that new belief was delivered by an angel. The apostle Paul anticipated such claims when he wrote that "even if we or an angel from heaven should preach a gospel other than the one we preached to you, let him be eternally condemned!" (Galatians 1:8; Colossians 2:18). Unfortunately, deceptive spiritual experiences and lying spirits are a reality in this world (1 John 4:1–2).

Jesus Christ is God's ultimate revelation to the world (Hebrews 1:1–2), with the New Testament being God's inspired "commentary" or "footnotes" explaining the meaning of the coming of Christ. No superior revelation, no better religion, and no greater person will ever come along than Jesus Christ. Christ is "far above all rule and authority, power and dominion, and every title that can be given, not only in the present age but also in the one to come" (Ephesians 1:21).

This means that no prophet, such as Muhammad, can offer a revelation of God that supersedes the revelation we have in Christ. It also means that any alleged prophet who claims to be "restoring" the gospel of Christ, such as Joseph Smith, must be put to the test of faithfulness to the New Testament.

C.C.A. Christensen (1831–1912), *The Hill Cumorah*.
Joseph Smith receives the golden plates from Moroni.

You should also know....

Others have started worldwide religious movements based on supposed angelic visitations. For example, William Branham—who denied the Trinity and distorted other important Christian doctrines—claimed that he was commissioned as God's end-time messenger by an angel in a "secret cave." Branham described the angel as a "huge man" with bare feet and an "olive complexion" who accompanied him (unseen by the public) throughout his miracle-working ministry, at one point indicating that the angel was Jesus himself.[19]

8 Q: Will angel encounters make you feel good?

Many people say...

You know it's an angel if it's comforting.
Some teachers, especially New Agers, encourage a wide-eyed openness to angelic experiences. Rarely will they admit that reported angelic encounters were either projections of the person's imagination or (worse still) encounters with evil spirits.

Doreen Virtue lists criteria for people to use to distinguish genuine angels from other experiences. A real angelic experience, she says, will "feel warm and cuddly," giving one a comforting feeling. "A deep belief that 'this is real'" is also a good sign. An authentic angelic encounter will "feel natural." An angelic encounter should be "positive and empowering," "energize you," and "ring true and make sense." Angels usually begin their sentences "with the words *you* or *me*," give you "a sense that someone else is talking to you," "ask you to take immediate action," and may be accompanied by "strains of beautiful, disembodied 'celestial' music."[20]

The Bible says...

"Warm fuzzies" don't prove that an experience is good—let alone that it comes from a holy angel of God. We need to keep in mind that even "Satan himself masquerades as an angel of light. It is not surprising, then, if his servants masquerade as servants of righteousness" (2 Corinthians 11:14–15).

Though it's hard to prove that someone's private angel encounter was real, the Bible helps us recognize when such claims are false (either the person's imagination or a demonic spirit). True angels from God:

• Glorify Jesus Christ (Luke 2:11; Hebrews 1:6).

• Give messages that never conflict with the apostles' teaching in the Bible (Galatians 1:8; 2 Corinthians 11:14; 1 Timothy 4:1; 1 John 4:1).

• Do not introduce new doctrines or practices into Christianity (Ephesians 2:19–20, 3:5; Jude 3).

• Do not offer assurance of salvation or spiritual comfort to those who don't believe in Christ, since those blessings come only from Christ (Romans 5:1–11; Ephesians 1:4–14).

You should also know....

Granted, it's easier to challenge reports of angel encounters than it is to prove them. But this shouldn't bother Christians, though, because no major biblical doctrine depends solely on the testimony of an angel. We may conclude that someone actually saw an angel *if their experience was consistent with Scripture,* but we must still be careful not to give such reports too much importance or emphasis.

© Amy Nichole Harris

Should you be on a first-name basis with angels?

Many people say...

Angels are ready to be our friends. Angel enthusiast Terry Lynn Taylor says, "Basically, I'm suggesting that you become best friends with your guardian angel! Pretend you have an invisible best friend who witnesses everything you experience and with whom you can share insights."[21]

According to author Eileen Elias Freeman, "Angels want to be our friends. They are companions on the journey of life on this planet, ancient fellow travelers, whose love and light and wisdom can enrich our lives immeasurably."[22] "Apostolic-prophetic" minister Steven Brooks urges Christians to develop relationships with "our friends, the angels."[23]

Doreen Virtue writes, "One way to get to know your angels even better is to ask them their names."[24] Rock musician Carlos Santana has done just that, and claims that since 1994 he's been in touch with an angel named Metatron who resembles Santa Claus ("white beard, and kind of this jolly fellow") and operates as his "inner voice."[25]

The Bible says...

Angels are not "friends," but Jesus Christ is. In fact, Jesus is the best friend we could hope for. Jesus—

Is our loyal friend: Jesus Christ said, "I will never leave you or forsake you." Heb. 13:5

Has chosen us as friends: "I have called you friends … I chose you." John 15:15–16

Forgives us: "He forgives all of our sins." Colossians 2:13

Saves us: "Believe on the Lord Jesus Christ and you will be saved." Acts 16:30–31

Makes everything work out well in the end: "And we know that God causes all things to work together for good to those who love God, to those who are called according to his purpose." Romans 8:28

Gives us new life: "If anyone is in Christ, he is a new creation." 2 Corinthians 5:17

Makes us his beloved children: "See how great a love the Father has bestowed upon us, that we should be called children of God." 1 John 3:1–2

Scripture makes it clear that the only supernatural being to whom we should pray and call upon is the Lord (Matthew 6:9). No one in the Bible ever calls on an angel, prays to an angel, asks God for an angel, or calls an angel a "friend."

You should also know....

Today's intense interest in having angels as companions and friends may reflect one of these misleading views of God:

• Many people believe that angels and saints are more tender-hearted or approachable than either the Father or the Son. This is sad, since God's love revealed in Christ is beyond any comparison (John 3:16; 15:9–13; Romans 5:8; Ephesians 5:1–2). God encourages believers to call on him as *Abba* (Aramaic: "Papa"), and he invites them to "approach [his] throne of grace with confidence" in their time of need (Romans 8:14–17; Hebrews 4:16).

• Angel enthusiasts often promote the New Age view of God as the divine "All"—that God is everything, or that everything is in some way part of God (called *pantheism*). But the Bible teaches that God is the personal Creator of the universe and that we and the angels are his creatures (Genesis 1:1; Psalm 100:3; Romans 1:25).

10 Q: Is Jesus just an angel?

Many people say...

Jesus is Michael the archangel. Some religious groups, most notably Jehovah's Witnesses, believe that Jesus was not God, but Michael the archangel. According to their *Watchtower* magazine, "The foremost angel, both in power and authority, is the archangel, Jesus Christ, also called Michael."[26] They argue that Paul's statement that the Lord Jesus will descend from heaven "with the voice of the archangel" (1 Thessalonians 4:16) shows that Jesus *is* the archangel.

Since Michael is called "the archangel" in Jude 9, Jehovah's Witnesses conclude that Jesus is in fact Michael. They also believe that the "angel of Jehovah" (or "angel of the LORD") in the Old Testament also is a description of Christ as a created angel.

The Bible says...

Jesus Christ is *not* Michael the archangel. Daniel 10:13 describes Michael as "one of the chief princes," indicating that he was a high-ranking angel, but not the ruler over all the angels. (The term "archangel" means chief angel.) Michael was an angel given a special assignment to protect Israel (Daniel 10:21; 12:1). Christ, on the other hand, is the one who made the angels (Colossians 1:16) and to whom all the angels give worship (Hebrews 1:6; Revelation 5:13–14). Jesus is infinitely superior to the angels (see the chart "Comparing Jesus and the Angels").

Paul says, "The Lord himself will come down from heaven, with a loud command, with the voice of the archangel and with the trumpet call of God" (1 Thessalonians 4:16). The idea here is that an archangel will announce the Lord's descent, not that the Lord is an archangel or that he personally has an archangel's voice. (It would be very odd to say that Christ himself had "the voice of the archangel" if he *were* the archangel!)

According to Jude 9, Michael the archangel refused to pronounce judgment against the Devil but deferred judgment to the Lord. The Lord who will judge the Devil, his fallen angels, and all other creatures is the Lord Jesus (Matthew 25:31–33; John 5:22–23; Revelation 20:7–15).

You should also know....

The term *angel* in both Hebrew and Greek means "messenger," and usually, but not always, refers to created spirit beings who serve as messengers of God (Hebrews 1:7, 14). It's possible that the "angel of the LORD" in the Old Testament refers to Christ (before he became a man) as the messenger of God the Father. This is consistent with the Christian belief in Jesus as God (the Son), since the Old Testament often speaks of the angel of the LORD as if he were the Lord God himself (Genesis 16:10–13; 22:11–12; 32:24–30; Exodus 3:1–8; 23:20–25; Judges 2:1–3; 6:11–27; 13:3–22). Most Christians in church history have regarded these passages as referring to *theophanies*—that is, appearances of God, specifically the person of the pre-incarnate Son of God (John 8:56–59; 1 Corinthians 10:4, 9; Jude 4–5).

Comparing Jesus and the Angels

JESUS	ANGELS
Creator of all things, including the angels (John 1:3; Col. 1:16; Heb. 1:2, 10)	Created beings (Nehemiah 9:6; Psalms 103:19–22; 148:25)
God—divine by nature (John 1:1; 20:28; Colossians 1:15–17; 2:9; Titus 2:13; Hebrews 1:3, 8; 2 Peter 1:1)	Not divine by nature, but mere created spirit servants of God (Hebrews 1:7, 14)
Died on the cross and rose from the grave to redeem us from sin and death (John 3:16; Romans 5:8)	Announced to the women at the tomb that Jesus had risen as he said he would (Matthew 28:56)
Christians are to put faith in him (John 14:1; 20:30-31; Romans 10:11), revere him (Ephesians 5:21; 1 Peter 3:15), and love him (John 14:15, 21; Ephesians 6:24)	Christians are *not* told to put faith in angels, to revere them, or to love them
Worshiped by all angels and all the redeemed forever (Hebrews 1:6; Revelation 5:13–14)	Worship Jesus Christ (Hebrews 1:6) and refuse human worship (Revelation 19:10; 22:89)
Sits on the very throne of God (Revelation 22:1–3)	Worship God and Christ around the throne (Revelation 5:13–14)
Has the name above every name—far above the angels (Ephesians 1:20–21; Philippians 2:9–11; Hebrews 1:4)	Most of their names are unknown to us, and all angels are Christ's humble servants (Hebrews 1:7, 14)

Terms for Heavenly Beings

BIBLE TERM	DEFINITION
Spirits	General term for supernatural beings without bodies.
Angels ("Messengers")	Spirits sent as messengers or agents from God; evil or fallen angels serve the Devil. Not often described; sometimes appear in white robes or as bright light.
Cherubim (Singular: Cherub)	Heavenly winged beings that fiercely guard the tree of life, the ark of the covenant, the temple, and the heavenly throne room.
Seraphim ("Burning One")	Heavenly winged guards in God's throne room.
Archangels ("Chief Princes")	Chief or ruling angels. Michael is the only archangel named in Scripture.
Thrones, powers, rulers, authorities, dominions	Spiritual beings that rule—typically for evil—over human affairs.

For Further Reading
The inclusion of a work does not necessarily mean endorsement of all its contents or of other works by the same author(s).

Angels among Us by Ron Rhodes (Harvest House, 1994)

Angels (and Demons): What Do We Really Know about Them? by Peter Kreeft (Ignatius, 1995) (Catholic)

Angels and the New Spirituality by Duane Garrett (Broadman & Holman, 1995)

The Angels and Us by Mortimer Adler (Macmillan, 1982)

Angels: God's Secret Agents by Billy Graham (Thomas Nelson, 2000)

The Gospel According to Angels by Robert W. Graves (Chosen, 1998)

Sense and Nonsense about Angels and Demons by Kenneth D. Boa and Robert M. Bowman, Jr. (Zondervan, 2007)

Notes:

1 Sylvia Browne, *Secret Societies* (Hay House, 2007), 155–176.

2 Doreen Virtue, "The Angel Guidance Board" (Hay House, 2005). (amazon.com author review).

3 John Randolph Price, *The Angels within Us* (Fawcett Columbine, 1993), 4.

4 Marilynn Carlson Webber and William D. Webber, *A Rustle of Angels* (Zondervan, 1994), 48.

5 Steven W. Brooks, *Working with Angels* (Destiny Image, 2007), 38.

6 Kevin Sullivan, *Wrestling with Angels* (Brill, 2004), 183–184.

7 Emanuel Swedenborg, *Heaven and Hell* (1758), trans. George F. Dole (Swedenborg Foundation, 2000), §§311, 315.

8 Doctrine & Covenants 129:1.

9 *Encyclopedia of Mormonism* (Macmillan, 1992) 1:39–40.

10 Hugh Pope, "Guardian Angel," *Catholic Encyclopedia* (Appleton, 1910).

11 Doreen Virtue, *Angel Visions* (Hay House, 2000), 161.

12 Karen Goldman, *The Angel Book* (Simon & Schuster, 1993), 20.

13 Charles and Frances Hunter, *The Angel Book* (Whitaker House, 1999), 121.

14 Linda Stover Van Fleet, "Faith," *I Believe in Angels!* (8 December 2004) (emphasis in original).

15 Silver Ravenwolf, *Angels: Companions in Magick* (Llewellyn, 1996), 111–112, x, 4.

16 Doreen Virtue, *Divine Prescriptions* (Renaissance, 2000), 43, 272.

17 C.T.R. Hewer, *Understanding Islam: An Introduction* (Fortress, 2006), 29.

18 Joseph Smith—History 1:30–65 in *Pearl of Great Price*

19 *Footprints in the Sands of Time* (Spoken Word Publications, 1975), 73–75, 79–80. *Twentieth Century Prophet* (video n.d.)

20 Doreen Virtue, *How to Hear Your Angels* (Hay House, 2007), 47–56.

21 Terry Lynn Taylor, *Guardians of Hope* (H.J. Kramer, 1993), 13.

22 Eileen Elias Freeman, *Angelic Healing* (Warner Books, 1994), xi–xii.

23 Steven Brooks, *Working with Angels* (Destiny Image, 2007) 90.

24 Doreen Virtue, *Angels 101* (Hay House, 2006), 24–25.

25 Chris Heath, "The Epic Life of Carlos Santana," *Rolling Stone* (March 2000).

26 "The Truth about Angels," *Watchtower* (1 November 1995), 8.

Principal Author: Robert M. Bowman, Jr., Director of the Institute for Religious Research (IRR), MA in Biblical Studies and Theology

General Editor: Paul Carden, Executive Director, Centers for Apologetics Research (CFAR)

Myths about Jesus

Myth: Jesus probably didn't exist.

Myth: Jesus was trained by gurus in the East.

Myth: Jesus was married.

Myth: Jesus didn't actually die on the cross.

Introduction

Since the 18th century, a number of scholars have questioned the testimony of the Gospels about Jesus. Today, many people are familiar with some of the criticisms these scholars raise. The issues are explored in books, articles, web sites, even television shows and movies. The criticisms have been repeated so often that many people accept them without question. Since most people are not trained in philosophy, theology, or history, the issues may seem to be mere matters of opinion.

In the following pages we will explore some of the most common misconceptions, which we call myths, about Jesus. The purpose is to provide information and insight about the origin, reasoning, and validity of some of these popular ideas. Although some arguments and historical evidence are presented, this work is not a formal dialogue with experts in the field. Rather, it is an introductory resource for believers who may be struggling with some of these questions, or people who are exploring the Christian faith but still have doubts.

A brief word about the historical reliability of the New Testament may be helpful. Modern science does not really prove or disprove miracles. However, history, archaeology, and other social sciences have shown the New Testament to be historically accurate and reliable. These are a few of the reasons for this confidence:

➤ The New Testament writings were based on eyewitness testimony.

➤ There are many documents from writers as early as the late first century AD which confirm various details of the New Testament accounts.

➤ The existence of many early manuscripts allows us to be confident that the New Testament was accurately copied.

Ancient walls of Jerusalem

Is Jesus of Nazareth a real person?

MYTH: Jesus probably didn't exist.

Some people argue that Jesus either did not exist or was so unlike the person described in the New Testament that we cannot know anything about him. "Historically, it is quite doubtful whether Christ ever existed at all, and if He did we do not know anything about Him" (Bertrand Russell, philosopher). "It is easier to account for the facts of early Christian history if Jesus were a fiction than if he once were real" (Frank R. Zindler, atheist activist).

FACT: Historical data confirm that the Gospel testimonies are reliable and accurate.

Historians agree that Jesus existed. Robert J. Miller, a skeptical historian, writes, "We can be certain that Jesus really existed (despite a few hyper-historical skeptics who refuse to be convinced)." Biblical scholar F. F. Bruce stated, "The historicity of Christ is as axiomatic [certain, unchallenged fact] for an unbiased historian as the historicity of Julius Caesar."

Many historical documents from around the time Jesus lived confirm the existence of Jesus. Along with the New Testament, there are references to Jesus in the writings of first-century and early second-century writers, such as Josephus (Jewish) and Tacitus and Pliny the Younger (Roman). No ancient writer who was opposed to Christianity questioned the historical existence of Jesus. The abundant data from the first century makes it highly possible—more than could be said of many other historical events—that the New Testament testimony is accurate.

Evidence from the Bible

Luke claimed that his Gospel was based on information handed down from "eyewitnesses" and on his own careful investigation (Luke 1:1–4). Likewise, the Gospel of John claims to be written by the very "disciple whom Jesus loved" (John 21:20–25; see also 2 Peter 1:16). Biblical authors understood the difference between history and myth, between fact and legend; they insisted that what they taught was literal, historical fact (see also 1 Corinthians 15:1–11; 2 Timothy 4:3–4).

Writing some twenty years after Jesus died, the apostle Paul mentions the following information about Jesus:

- Jesus' twelve apostles, specifically Peter (Cephas), James, and John (1 Corinthians 15:5, 7; Galatians 1:8–9).
- The Last Supper (1 Corinthians 11:23–26).
- Jesus' death and burial (1 Corinthians 15:3–4; 1 Thessalonians 2:13–16).
- Jesus' resurrection and appearances (1 Corinthians 15:5–8).
- At least some of Jesus' teachings (e.g., 1 Corinthians 9:14; cf. Luke 10:7).

Do the "Gnostic gospels" tell the real story of Jesus?

MYTH: The Gnostic gospels provide new light on the historical Jesus.

In recent years, interest in the "lost gospels"—ancient books about Jesus not included in the New Testament—has increased dramatically, thanks to books and movies like *The Da Vinci Code*. However, since 1945, when most of these lost gospels were discovered, many scholars have looked to these gospels outside the New Testament for alternative views of Jesus. Some of these scholars claim that the lost gospels portray more accurately who Jesus was.

The most significant of these ancient writings are the Gnostic gospels, which reinterpreted Jesus' life and teaching more than a century after his death. The word "Gnostic" comes from the Greek word *gnosis* ("knowledge") and refers to the Gnostics' claim to have secret information about Jesus. Gnostics generally believed that one or more semi-divine beings inferior to the true God created the world and trapped spirits in physical bodies. They also believed that salvation consisted of using their secret knowledge to escape the physical realm and unite with God.

The controversial Jesus Seminar scholars included one of the lost gospels, the *Coptic Gospel of Thomas*, in their book *The Five Gospels*—and accepted more of its sayings of Jesus than those found in the Gospel of John.

FACT: The Gnostic gospels don't provide any helpful information about the historical Jesus.

The Gnostic gospels do not include eyewitness testimony about Jesus. The New Testament gospels appeared in the first century, while people who knew Jesus might still be alive; the Gnostic gospels came out in the second century or even later. All scholars agree that it is certain that Thomas, Peter, and Judas did not actually write the "gospels" that bear their names.

Moreover, the purpose of the Gnostic gospels was to communicate Gnostic beliefs—which contradict both the Old and New Testaments—rather than to convey concrete information about Jesus' life.

Evidence from the Bible

Since the Gnostic gospels appeared years later, there is no direct response to Gnostic claims about Jesus in the New Testament (though the epistles of Colossians and 1 John address ideas that the Gnostics developed more fully). But the New Testament writings did claim to have been based on the testimonies of eyewitnesses of Jesus' life, ministry, death, and resurrection (see Luke 1:1–4; John 19:35; 21:24–25; Acts 1:21–26; 10:36–42; 1 Corinthians 9:1; 15:3–8; Galatians 1:11–12; 1 John 1:1–4). Paul recognized that other interpretations of Jesus' life and identity would arise; he warned believers to be on guard (2 Corinthians 11:4).

Did the early church borrow the Virgin Birth story from paganism?

MYTH:
Pagan society had many stories of miraculous virgin births.

Some scholars, and even some people in the church, argue that the Virgin Birth is probably just a fictional legend.

James Tabor writes, "The assumption of the historian is that all human beings have both a biological mother and father, and that Jesus is no exception." Similarly, John Drury, Oxford University chaplain, remarks, "Virgin births were a rather Gentile thing. You get it in a lot of the legends in Ovid where the god impregnates some young girl who has a miraculous son."

FACT:
The birth of Jesus was a special, unique event in history.

Because of the very private nature of conception and pregnancy, it is impossible to prove the Virgin Birth historically. However, it is possible to show that there are good reasons to accept the event as historical fact.

Most importantly, the pagan stories are not about "virgin births" at all. As some scholars admit, in pagan stories the gods impregnated women by having sexual relations with them. Tabor agrees, "In that sense the account [in the Gospels] is different from those miraculous birth stories so common in Greco-Roman mythology." Skeptics like Gerd Lüdemann (an atheist scholar) and John Shelby Spong (the former Episcopal bishop of Newark), following the feminist scholar Jane Schaberg, take the view that Jesus was Mary's illegitimate child. However, the Gospels of Matthew and Luke, which report the Virgin Birth, were written in the first century—still within the lifetime of family members and others who had known Jesus personally.

Evidence from the Bible

"This is how the birth of Jesus Christ came about: his mother Mary was pledged to be married to Joseph, but before they came together, she was found to be with child through the Holy Spirit" (Matthew 1:18).

The dialogue between the angel and Mary in Luke 1:30–37 makes it clear that:

- Mary was a virgin.

- Jesus' birth was a special act of the Holy Spirit.

Orazio Gentleschi (1563-1639)–*Annunciation*

Where was Jesus during his "lost years"?

MYTH: Jesus was trained by gurus in the East.

People have often wondered why the New Testament does not offer more details about Jesus' life, especially between the ages of twelve and thirty. Some suggest that Jesus traveled far and wide during these so-called "lost years" to learn from other religious leaders.

At the end of the 18th century, a wealthy Russian explorer, Nicolas Notovitch, claimed to have discovered an ancient Buddhist manuscript. This manuscript described how Jesus lived and studied around India.

Today, some New Age teachers cite this story to support their claim that Jesus taught something more like Buddhism than Christianity. For example, actress and author Shirley MacLaine claims that Jesus was "traveling in and around India and Tibet and Persia and the Near East" and was trained as a "yogi" before returning to Galilee.

FACT: There is no basis in fact for the claim that Jesus studied in the East.

No ancient document—not even any of the "gospels" that were not included in the New Testament—affirms that Jesus ever lived or traveled outside the land of Israel, except for his infancy in Egypt (Matthew 2).

The most frequently cited source for the claim that Jesus went East is Notovitch's book *The Unknown Life of Jesus Christ*. Notovitch's claims were strongly questioned from the beginning. For example:

- During Jesus' lifetime, the main religion in Tibet was the Bön religion (a form of shamanism), not Buddhism.

- Although Notovitch did travel to Tibet, Archibald Douglas, a British professor, proved in 1895 that Notovitch had not visited the monastery in question.

- Douglas also showed that the monastery did not have a manuscript mentioning Jesus.

Evidence from the Bible

Although the Gospels do not report on Jesus' specific activities between the ages of twelve and thirty, they do tell us enough to discount the theory that Jesus was studying Buddhism in the East during those years.

The Gospels also report that people in Jesus' hometown of Nazareth knew him as a carpenter, a trade he learned from Joseph (Matthew 13:55; Mark 6:3), which suggests that Jesus spent his young adult years there. After his baptism and time in the desert, "Jesus returned to Galilee," went to Nazareth, "and on the Sabbath day he went into the synagogue, as was his custom" (Luke 4:14–16).

Can we become the Christ?

MYTH: Jesus was just a man who realized his "Christ consciousness."

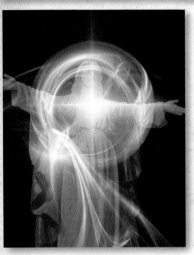

As some Eastern religions have become more influential in the West, many people have reinterpreted Christian terms using Eastern concepts. For example, the New Age movement and Mind-Science groups (such as Christian Science and Unity) interpret "Christ" to mean "the divine that is in all of us." In this view, Jesus was just a man who attained "Christ consciousness"—a realization of oneness with the divine that is the potential in all human beings. For example: "We are all manifestations of Buddha consciousness, or Christ consciousness, only we don't know it. The word 'Buddha' means 'the one who waked up.' We are all to do that—to wake up to the Christ or Buddha consciousness within us" (Joseph Campbell, professor of mythology).

FACT: Only Jesus qualifies to be "the Christ."

The title "Christ" (Greek, *christos*) means "anointed one." The "Christ" was the anointed king who would fulfill God's promises to David of an eternal kingdom of justice and peace through one of his descendants. Jesus, a descendant of David, claimed to be that anointed one (Luke 4:16–21). Although various individuals in the Old Testament (such as King David) were anointed to their offices, there could only be one divinely anointed king of God's people. Similarly, all believers are said to have an "anointing" from God (1 John 2:20–27), but the New Testament recognizes only Jesus as "the Christ."

The concept of a universal "Christ consciousness" is a modern creation; it may be compatible with some forms of Buddhism, but it is *not* a Christian idea.

Evidence from the Bible

Jesus said, "For many will come in my name, claiming, 'I am the Christ,' and will deceive many" (Matthew 24:5).

"The woman said, 'I know that Messiah' (called Christ) 'is coming. When he comes, he will explain everything to us.' Then Jesus declared, 'I who speak to you am he'" (John 4:25–26).

"But these are written that you may believe that Jesus is the Christ, the Son of God, and that by believing you may have life in his name" (John 20:31).

Was Jesus married?

MYTH: The church conspired to conceal Jesus' marriage.

The idea that Jesus was married became especially popular after Dan Brown's novel *The Da Vinci Code*, which claims, "The marriage of Jesus and Mary Magdalene is part of the historical record."

James Tabor argues that the silence of the Gospels about Jesus' wife is no more significant than their silence about the wives of Jesus' brothers and apostles: "They are simply not considered important to the story, but it does not mean they did not exist." Others argue that all Jewish rabbis were married, and therefore, since Jesus was a rabbi, he must have been married at some point.

Writers who claim that Jesus and Mary Magdalene were husband and wife think this is implied in some of the Gnostic gospels. For example, the *Gospel of Philip* (probably written in the third century AD) makes some sort of statement about Jesus kissing Mary, which many interpret as proof they were married.

FACT: There is no evidence that Jesus was married.

The arguments marshaled by proponents of this view do not support their case:

- Sections of the only existing copy of the *Gospel of Philip* are greatly damaged and difficult to read clearly. We should be hesitant to derive any confident conclusions from this fragmented sentence in a document dating two centuries after Jesus.

- Most scholars agree that the "kiss" here refers to a religious, mystical ritual of some sort involving a kiss.

- As scientist Charles Pellegrino (who claims that Jesus and Mary were married) admits: "In none of the Gospels, be they canonical or apocryphal, is Mary Magdalene—*Mariamne*—described as being married to Jesus."

- While rabbis generally frowned on men not marrying, they acknowledged that there could be exceptions, notably for prophets. Some groups of Jews at the time of Jesus (such as the Essenes) actually encouraged celibacy.

Evidence from the Bible

The Gospels mention many of Jesus' relatives, including father, mother, brothers, sisters, and cousins, but no wife or children. Their silence about whether Jesus was married, then, is at least good evidence that he was not.

The Bible makes it clear that Jesus' mission was to redeem people from sin so that they could become God's adopted children (Matthew 5:9; 6:9; 7:11; 23:8–9; Mark 3:33–35; Romans 8:14–23, 29; Galatians 4:4–7). He dedicated his life to this mission of redemption. Perhaps this is why Jesus did not get married and start a family.

Did Jesus die on the cross?

MYTH: Jesus somehow avoided——or survived——crucifixion.

A surprisingly large number of people in the world know something about Jesus but think that he did not really die on the cross.

According to the *Qur'an*, the scripture of Islam, the Jews claimed to have killed Jesus, but "they slew him not nor crucified him, but it appeared so unto them." Many Muslims think someone else—perhaps even Judas—was crucified instead.

Others agree that Jesus was crucified but speculate that he survived the ordeal, perhaps merely passing out on the cross (the "swoon theory"). Conspiracy theorist Michael Baigent asserts that when Mark reports that Joseph of Arimathea asked Pilate permission to bury Jesus' "body," Mark uses the Greek word *soma*—which, he claims, means a live body, not a corpse (Mark 15:43). Baigent concludes: "Jesus' survival is revealed right there in the Gospel account."

FACT: Jesus died on the cross.

Caravaggio (1571–1610)—*The Entombment*

The claim that someone other than Jesus died on the cross has no historical evidence to support it. Friends and family members, including his mother Mary, witnessed his crucifixion (Luke 23:49–56; John 19:25–27, 38–42). The Jewish leaders had seen Jesus in Jerusalem for several days, and they would certainly have known and objected if the Romans were crucifying the wrong man.

Baigent is mistaken: the word *soma* can refer either to a live body or to a corpse (for example, Luke 17:37; Acts 9:40; Romans 8:10). The swoon theory picks and chooses select elements of the Gospel accounts and takes them out of context:

- Pilate was surprised that Jesus had perished so quickly (Mark 15:44a), since crucifixion victims usually took days to die. However, Mark also tells us that Pilate checked with the centurion who oversaw Jesus' execution and verified that he was in fact dead (15:44b–45).

- When a soldier pierced Jesus' body with a spear, "blood and water came out" (John 19:34), supposedly proving that he was still alive. Medical experts have offered several suggestions as to the source of the blood and water, all consistent with Jesus' already being dead. In any case, had Jesus not quite been dead, stabbing him with a spear so that he lost still more blood would surely have finished the job.

Even skeptic and scholar John Dominic Crossan has stated: "Jesus' death by execution under Pontius Pilate is as sure as anything historical can ever be."

Did archaeologists find Jesus' bones?

MYTH: The "Jesus family tomb" belonged to Jesus.

Simcha Jacobovici, a journalist specializing in biblical archaeological news, and Charles Pellegrino, a science writer, claimed in 2007 that they had found the tomb in which Jesus, his mother Mary, brother Joseph, wife Mary Magdalene, and son Judah were buried.

Israeli authorities warehouse hundreds of ossuaries—limestone boxes in which first-century Jews buried the dried-out bones of the deceased. Among the ossuaries found in a tomb in Talpiot (a Jerusalem suburb) were ones inscribed with the names "Jesus son of Joseph," "Jose," "Maria," "Judah son of Jesus," "Matia," and one with a disputed inscription that some say reads "Mariamne also known as Mara." Jacobovici and Pellegrino claim this means "Mary the Master" and identify her as Mary Magdalene, whom some Christians regarded as a spiritual authority.

Jacobovici and Pellegrino concluded that the Talpiot tomb was the final resting place of the bones of Jesus Christ.

FACT: The tomb doesn't belong to Jesus or his family.

Despite the popularity of the idea, virtually no biblical scholar (other than James Tabor) has endorsed the "Jesus family tomb" theory. One of the main reasons is that "Jesus" and "Joseph" were very common names in the first century, as was "Mary" (about one out of four women had that name).

The "Jesus family tomb" theory depends largely on identifying one of the Marys as Mary Magdalene, but this is the argument's weakest point. The inscription either says "Mary also known as Mara" or "Mary and Mara"—and Mara was another name for Martha. In this context, the meaning "Master" is highly unlikely. And no ancient text calls Mary Magdalene a "Master." Since we are reasonably sure Jesus Christ did not have a wife or son, we can confidently reject the Talpiot tomb as belonging to him.

Evidence from the Bible

The Gospels report that Jesus' body was buried in the tomb of Joseph of Arimathea in the late afternoon before the Sabbath (Mark 15:42–47). Early on the morning of the Sabbath, several of his women followers went to the tomb to anoint the body and discovered the tomb empty. An angel at the tomb told the women, "Don't be alarmed.... You are looking for Jesus the Nazarene, who was crucified. He has risen! He is not here. See the place where they laid him" (Mark 16:6).

Joseph's tomb was empty because Jesus had risen from the dead, not because his body had been moved to another tomb.

Did Jesus rise from the grave?

MYTH: The resurrection of Jesus is merely a pious legend.

Skeptics discount the resurrection of Jesus as a miracle—and they typically reject the possibility of miracles altogether.

"If you say that Jesus rose from the dead biologically, you would have to presuppose that a decaying corpse—which is already cold and without blood in its brain—could be made alive again. I think that is nonsense" (Gerd Lüdemann, professor of early Christianity).

The belief that Jesus rose physically from the dead "is exactly like the belief in Santa's visiting every child's home throughout the earth during a single evening" (Robert M. Price, professor of theology).

FACT: The available evidence strongly suggests that Jesus' resurrection was a fact.

If Jesus' resurrection were a legend, the Jewish authorities would not have accused Jesus' disciples of having stolen the body. Hundreds of people personally saw the risen Jesus. These eyewitnesses suffered persecution and, in some cases, martyrdom for these stories.

To reject the possibility of miracles is to make a philosophical assumption, not something that skeptics can prove through science or history. Skeptical explanations (such as the "swoon theory" or the claim the disciples suffered a mass hallucination) simply do not work. In the words of New Testament scholar N.T. Wright, "Once you allow that something remarkable happened to the body that morning, all the other data fall into place with ease. Once you insist that nothing so outlandish happened, you are driven to ever more complex and fantastic hypotheses."

The best explanation for all of the known facts is that Jesus did in fact rise from the dead.

Evidence from the Bible

The Gospels report that Jesus died, that he was buried in a rock tomb, and that women followers of Jesus discovered the tomb to be empty a couple of days later (Matt. 28:1–7), a fact confirmed by male followers (Luke 24:12; John 20:3–10). Jesus appeared alive to some of those same women (Matthew 28:8–10; John 20:11–18). He also appeared to his apostles (Luke 24:34; 1 Corinthians 15:5, 7; Matthew 28:16–20; Luke 24:36–49; John 20:19–29). On one occasion he appeared to more than five hundred (1 Corinthians 15:6). He even appeared to Saul (Paul), a rabbi who had fiercely opposed the Christian faith (Acts 9:1-9; 1 Corinthians 15:8).

Is Jesus the only way to God?

MYTH: Jesus is merely one of the world's many religious leaders.

Many people argue that while belief in Jesus is fine for some, it is intolerant—even hateful—to say that Jesus is the only way to know God, the only way of salvation.

Oprah Winfrey, in response to a member of her studio audience who argued that Jesus was the only way to God, replied, "There couldn't *possibly* be only one way."

New Age teacher Deepak Chopra claims, "I want to offer the possibility that Jesus was truly, as he proclaimed, a savior. Not the savior, not the one and only Son of God. Rather, Jesus embodied the highest level of enlightenment."

FACT: Jesus claimed to be the exclusive way to God and salvation.

If Jesus had been merely a religious and ethical teacher, he might even have been the best such teacher—but by no means the only one. When people criticize the notion that Jesus is the only way, they are typically thinking of Jesus as a teacher or guru, an enlightened master or a spiritual role model. However, this is not an adequate understanding of who or what Jesus is. Jesus made claims about himself and performed wonders that no one else did:

1. He is the Son of God.

2. He lived a sinless life, raised the dead, gave sight to the blind.

3. He died as a substitute for the sins of the world, so that we may have eternal life in God's kingdom.

4. He will be the Judge at the end of history, determining who receives eternal life and who does not.

These claims are either extremely arrogant and delusional, or true.

Evidence from the Bible

"Jesus answered, 'I am the way and the truth and the life. No one comes to the Father except through me'" (John 14:6).

"Salvation is found in no one else, for there is no other name under heaven given to men by which we must be saved" (Acts 4:12).

"Therefore God exalted him to the highest place and gave him the name that is above every name, that at the name of Jesus every knee should bow, in heaven and on earth and under the earth, and every tongue confess that Jesus Christ is Lord, to the glory of God the Father" (Philippians 2:9–11).

Is Jesus God?

The New Testament teaches that Jesus is God:

- It explicitly refers to him as "God" (John 1:1; 20:28; Titus 2:13; Hebrews 1:8; 2 Peter 1:1).

- It gives him other divine titles, such as "Lord"—often in contexts where this title clearly stands for the Old Testament name Yahweh (Romans 10:9–13, see Joel 2:32; Philippians 2:9–11; Isaiah 45:23).

- Jesus is the King of kings and Lord of lords (Revelation 17:14; 19:16; see Daniel 4:37).

- He is the first and the last, the beginning and the end, the Alpha and Omega (Revelation 1:7–8, 17b–18; 2:8; 22:13–14; see Isaiah 41:4; 44:6; 48:12).

- It describes him as having divine attributes, such as having no beginning (John 1:1–3; Colossians 1:16–17), existing everywhere at the same time (Matthew 18:20; 28:20), and being absolutely loving (Romans 8:35–39; Ephesians 3:19).

- It credits him with doing God's works, such as creating and sustaining the world (John 1:3; Colossians 1:16–17; Hebrews 1:2–3, 10). Jesus forgave sins (Mark 2:1–12) and claimed that he will pass final judgment on all people (John 5:22–23).

- It accords all divine honors to him (John 5:23): worship (Matthew 28:17; Hebrews 1:6), prayer (John 14:14; 1 Corinthians 1:2; Revelation 22:20–21), and reverence (Ephesians 5:21).

Principal Author: Robert M. Bowman, Jr., Director of the Institute for Religious Research (IRR), MA in Biblical Studies and Theology

General Editor: Paul Carden, Executive Director, Centers for Apologetics Research (CFAR)

Did Jesus Rise from the Dead?
Reasons to Believe in the Resurrection

> **1** The reliability for the resurrection is supported by many witnesses.

Skeptics claim that there were no impartial witnesses who could verify the physical resurrection of Jesus Christ.

All four gospels agree that the first eyewitnesses to the proof of Jesus' resurrection were women. Anyone wishing to make up a story in the first century would not use women as their primary witnesses. On the surface, this does not seem like a major proof for the resurrection. Some may argue that these women, who were very close to Jesus, are not objective witnesses. But the significance of these eyewitnesses lies in understanding the role of women in first century Judea.

During the time of Jesus, a woman's testimony was considered worthless. In fact, a woman was not allowed to serve as a witness in court. If early believers wanted to fabricate the resurrection, they would have come up with witnesses who were men who had political and religious influence in their community. Instead, the writers reported the actual witnesses who were women and also close friends of Jesus. Those who recorded these events wanted to be accurate.

No one ever produced the body of Jesus. "In 56 AD Paul wrote that over 500 people had seen the risen Jesus and that most of them were still alive (1 Corinthians 15:6). It passes the bounds of credibility that the early Christians could have manufactured such a tale and then preached it among those who might easily have refuted it simply by producing the body of Jesus."[3] The greatest weapon against these early eyewitnesses would have been to produce the

© Glenda M. Powers

body of Jesus. That weapon was never used, because it didn't exist. The silence of those who opposed Christianity while Jesus' followers preached about the empty tomb only confirmed the fact that the tomb really was empty and its vacancy could not be explained otherwise.

2   People will not knowingly die for a lie.

Skeptics claim that after Jesus died his followers invented a plan to deceive the entire world into believing that Jesus was the promised Messiah who rose from the dead.

Evidence suggests that such a deception is highly unlikely. The disciples were not fearless liars who wanted to fool the world. After the crucifixion, the disciples fled in fear for their lives. However, once they saw, touched, and spoke with the risen Lord, their lives were transformed. The disciples left their former jobs and entered a life of telling about Jesus, and as a result, they endured hunger persecution, abandonment, imprisonment, suffering, torture, and death. "People will die for their religious beliefs if they sincerely believe they're true, but people won't die for their religious beliefs if they know their beliefs are false."[1]

All of Jesus' followers doubted the resurrection until Jesus physically appeared to them—then they believed.

- The women at the empty tomb were afraid and thought someone had stolen the body. Once Jesus appeared, the women worshiped him and shared the news with the disciples (Matthew 28:1–10).
- The disciples did not believe the women's report of the empty tomb. They did not believe until Jesus appeared before them.
- Thomas did not trust the testimony of the other disciples. He wanted to see and touch Jesus in order to believe. Once he did see Jesus, he believed.
- James, the brother of Jesus, was embarrassed of Jesus during Jesus' ministry (Matthew 13:55–56). However, after encountering the risen Lord (1 Corinthians 15:7), James became the leader of the Jerusalem church and, according to Josephus, was stoned to death because of his faith.[2]
- Saul was a Pharisee who strongly opposed Christians, so much so, that he persecuted believers and assisted in the execution of early Christians. When the risen Christ appeared to Saul on the Damascus road, Saul was completely transformed. Saul, also known as Paul, became one of the greatest followers of Jesus. Throughout his lifetime, he was continuously persecuted and imprisoned for preaching the good news of Jesus. Paul's letters to churches and pastors comprise 13 books of the New Testament.

3   Sociological evidence suggests that the resurrection was a historical event.

Skeptics claim that the physical resurrection was not very important to the early church because Christianity began as a moral and philosophical movement.

The drastic social change in faithful Jews is evidence of the resurrection. For thousands of years, Jews endured persecution, oppression, and were scattered over the face of the earth. Unlike every culture around them, the Jewish people never lost their cultural and religious identity. Only a few years after the crucifixion, more than 10,000 Jews embraced the teachings of Jesus Christ and his followers. These early Jewish Christians continued to worship on the Sabbath, but they began worshiping on Sundays as well to mark the resurrection of Christ. As the church matured, they continued to worship on Sundays and referred to those days as "Little Easters." One reasonable explanation for the transformation of so many Jews is that they, or people they knew, had seen Jesus Christ after he rose from the dead.

Early church practices celebrated the resurrection. Jesus' followers were baptized when they first believed and then they would gather together to celebrate the Lord's Supper.

- Baptism celebrates the death and resurrection of Christ (Colossians 2:12). "We were therefore buried with him through baptism into death in order that, just as Christ was raised from the dead through the glory of the Father, we too may live a new life" (Romans 6:4).
- In the Lord's Supper, believers eat bread and drink wine as a memorial to the suffering and death of Christ, as Jesus requested before he died. The Scriptures suggest that the Lord's Supper is a time of joy (Luke 24:30–35; Hebrews 12:2). There is joy because believers recognize that with the crucifixion there is death, but with the resurrection there is eternal life.

These two practices would not have been carried out if the resurrection had not been a central component to the Christian faith.

4   Alternative theories don't pass scrutiny.

The Hallucination Theory: *All of the appearances of Jesus after his death were hallucinations.*

This is not true because:
- More than 500 people could not have the same hallucination. "Hallucinations are individual occurrences. By their very nature only one person can see a given hallucination at a time."[4]

- Those who saw Jesus after his death did not expect to see him and were surprised by his being there. Psychiatrists state that hallucinations require expectation.[5]

The "Swoon" Theory: *Jesus fainted while on the cross, then was removed and placed in a tomb. Later, Jesus was revived and left the tomb in a weakened condition.*

If this were true, then:
- Jesus had to survive massive blood loss, torture, and a stab wound in his side.
- The Roman soldiers, who were well acquainted with crucifixion, would have failed in their duties, thus facing the penalty of execution themselves.
- The soldiers broke the legs of the two criminals crucified next to Jesus in order to speed up their death. If Jesus were still alive, they would have done the same to him.
- When Jesus was stabbed in the side, water mixed with blood poured out, medically indicating that Jesus had already died.
- Every eyewitness of his death would have been mistaken.
- Jesus had to roll the massive tombstone away, sneak past the soldiers, and walk several miles on the road to Emmaus.

The Stolen Body Theory: *Jesus' disciples came by night and stole Jesus' body while the soldiers slept.*

This is not true because:
- Matthew's Gospel reports that the soldiers were bribed by the Jewish priests and elders in order to keep the truth a secret (Matthew 28:13–15).
- The enemies of Jesus took steps to prevent the disciples from stealing the body, such as sealing the stone and providing a guard of soldiers to watch the tomb.
- The soldiers at the tomb would not sleep for fear of failing in their duties and thus suffering the death penalty.
- During the crucifixion the disciples cowardly abandoned Jesus. They would not have had the courage to pass by the guard, silently move the massive stone, rob the grave, and leave undetected.

The Wrong Tomb Theory: *Every person who witnessed the empty tomb was peering into the wrong tomb. Jesus' body was in a different location.*

This is not true because:
- The women observed where Jesus' body was laid only a few days earlier.
- If Jesus' body were still in its correct tomb, his enemies could have produced the body immediately.
- If everyone went to the wrong tomb, Joseph of Arimathea, the owner of the tomb, would have corrected them.

Notes

Q 1: Bertrand Russell, "Why I Am Not a Christian," in *Why I Am Not a Christian and Other Essays on Religion and Related Subjects* (Touchstone, 1967), 16; Frank R. Zindler, "Did Jesus Exist?" *American Atheist*, Summer 1998; F. F. Bruce, *The New Testament Documents: Are They Reliable?* (IVP, 1960), 119. Robert J. Miller, "Back to Basics: A Primer on Historical Method," in *Finding the Historical Jesus: Rules of Evidence*, ed. Bernard Brandon Scott, Jesus Seminar Guides (Santa Rosa, CA: Polebridge Press, 2008), 10.

Q 3: James D. Tabor, *The Jesus Dynasty* (Simon & Schuster, 2006), 59, 45; John Drury, quoted in *Time*, 12/8/04; Gerd Lüdemann, *Virgin Birth?* (Trinity Press Intl., 1998), 51–65; Jane Schaberg, *The Illegitimacy of Jesus* (Harper, 1987).

Q 4: Shirley MacLaine, *Out on a Limb* (Bantam, 1984), 233–34; J. Archibald Douglas, "The Chief Lama of Himis on the Alleged 'Unknown Life of Christ,'" *The Nineteenth Century*, 39 (January-June 1896): 667–77.

Q 5: Joseph Campbell, *The Power of Myth*, with Bill Moyers (Anchor Books, 1991), 69.

Q 6: Dan Brown, *The Da Vinci Code* (Doubleday, 2003), 234, 245, 317; James Tabor, "Was Jesus Married?" (http://jesusdynasty.com/blog/); Simcha Jacobovici and Charles Pellegrino, *The Jesus Family Tomb* (HarperSanFrancisco, 2007), 105.

Q 7: Qur'an 4:157–58; Michael Baigent, *The Jesus Papers* (HarperCollins, 2006), 130; Matthew W. Maslen and Piers D. Mitchell, "Medical Theories on the Cause of Death in Crucifixion," *Journal of the Royal Society of Medicine* 99 (2006): 185–88; John Dominic Crossan, *Who Killed Jesus?* (Harper, 1995), 5.

Q 8: Jacobovici and Pellegrino, *Jesus Family Tomb*; James Tabor, http://jesusdynasty.com/blog/.

Q 9: *Jesus' Resurrection: Fact or Figment? A Debate Between William Lane Craig & Gerd Lüdemann*, ed. Paul Copan and Ronald K. Tacelli (IVP, 2000), 45; "Introduction," in *The Empty Tomb: Jesus Beyond the Grave*, ed. Robert M. Price and Jeffery Jay Lowder (Prometheus, 2005), 12; *The Meaning of Jesus: Two Visions*, by N. T. Wright and Marcus Borg (SPCK, 1999), 124.

Q 10: "The Gospel According to Oprah," www.wfial.org; Deepak Chopra, *The Third Jesus: The Christ We Cannot Ignore* (Harmony, 2008).

Reasons for Believing in the Resurrection:

1. Strobel, Lee, *The Case for Christ*, Grand Rapids, MI: Zondervan, 1998.
2. Josephus, *The Antiquities* 20.200.
3. Montgomery, John W., *History and Christianity*, Downers Grove, Ill.: InterVarsity Press, 1971.
4. Dr. Gary Collins cited in Lee Strobel, *The Case for Christ*, Grand Rapids, MI: Zondervan, 1998.
5. Corsinii, Raymond J. *Encyclopedia of Psychology, Vol 2*, New York, NY: John Wiley and Sons, Inc.. 2001.

Recommended Reading

Note: The inclusion of a work does not necessarily mean endorsement of all its contents or of other works by the same author(s).

Bauckham, Richard. *Jesus and the Eyewitnesses.* Eerdmans, 2006.

Blomberg, Craig L. *The Historical Reliability of the Gospels.* 2d ed. IVP, 2008.

Bock, Darrell L. *The Missing Gospels.* Thomas Nelson, 2007.

Bock, Darrell L., and Daniel B. Wallace. *Dethroning Jesus: Exposing Popular Culture's Quest to Unseat the Biblical Christ.* Thomas Nelson, 2007.

Bowman, Robert M., Jr., and J. Ed Komoszewski. *Putting Jesus in His Place: The Case for the Deity of Christ.* Kregel, 2007.

Bruce, F. F. *The New Testament Documents: Are They Reliable?* 6th ed. Eerdmans/IVP, 1981.

Eddy, Paul Rhodes, and Gregory A. Boyd. *The Jesus Legend: A Case for the Historical Reliability of the Synoptic Jesus Tradition.* Baker, 2007. Advanced study.

Edwards, James R. *Is Jesus the Only Savior?* Eerdmans, 2005.

Evans, Craig A. *Fabricating Jesus.* IVP, 2006.

Geivett, R. Douglas, and Gary R. Habermas, eds. *In Defense of Miracles.* IVP, 1997.

Groothuis, Douglas R. *Jesus in an Age of Controversy.* Wipf & Stock, 2002.

Habermas, Gary R., and Michael R. Licona. *The Case for the Resurrection of Jesus.* Kregel, 2004.

Hengel, Martin. *Crucifixion in the Ancient World and the Folly of the Message of the Cross.* Fortress, 1977. Advanced study.

Jenkins, Philip. *Hidden Gospels: How the Search for Jesus Lost Its Way.* Oxford, 2002.

Jones, Timothy Paul. *Misquoting Truth: A Guide to the Fallacies of Bart Ehrman's "Misquoting Jesus".* IVP, 2007.

Komoszewski, J. Ed, M. James Sawyer, and Daniel B. Wallace. *Reinventing Jesus.* Kregel, 2006.

Pate, C. Marvin, and Sheryl Lynn Pate. *Crucified in the Media: Finding the Real Jesus Amidst Today's Headlines.* Baker, 2005.

Quarles, Charles, ed. *Buried Hope or Risen Savior? The Search for the Jesus Tomb.* Broadman & Holman, 2008.

Roberts, Mark D. *Can We Trust the Gospels?* Crossway, 2007.

Strobel, Lee. *The Case for the Real Jesus.* Zondervan, 2007.

Van Voorst, Robert E. *Jesus Outside the New Testament.* Eerdmans, 2000. Advanced study.

Myths about the Bible

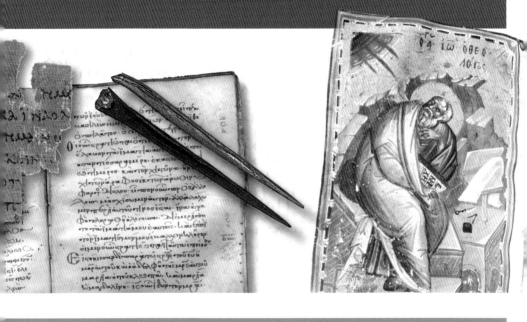

Myth: The Bible is filled with errors.

Myth: The Bible was tampered with.

Myth: The Gospel writers never even met Jesus.

Myth: Stories in the New Testament were made up.

Can the Bible Be Trusted?

Before the invention of the printing press, scribes copied the Scriptures by hand for more than one thousand years—

♦ without eyeglasses

♦ by the light of candles

♦ using quill pens and ground charcoal mixed with gum and water to scratch the sacred words of Scripture on rough papyrus and vellum

What if these scribes got it wrong?

Some recent bestselling books—such as Bart Ehrman's *Misquoting Jesus*—argue that the scribes *did* get it wrong. Here's a summary of recent claims about the surviving manuscripts of the Bible: "Not only do we not have the originals [of the biblical manuscripts], we don't have the first copies of the originals. We have only error-ridden copies, and the vast majority of these are centuries removed from the originals and different from them in thousands of ways. Mistakes multiply and get repeated; sometimes they get corrected and sometimes they get compounded. And so it goes. For centuries. In some places, we simply cannot be sure that we have reconstructed the text accurately. It's a bit hard to know what the words of the Bible mean if we don't even know what the words are."[1]

Thousands of people read and believe these attacks on the Bible. Still, millions of people continue to trust the Bible as an authoritative, written record that conveys consistent and reliable truth about God. So which is it?

Does the Bible still convey the truths that the original authors intended? Or were the ancient texts changed with such reckless abandon that contemporary biblical scholars are left with manuscripts so "error-ridden" they can't even be certain what the texts originally meant?

With these questions in mind, let's look at the history of the biblical texts to see what the historical record actually tells us!

Here's what we'll find:

♦ The Bible can be trusted.

♦ We can know what the Bible says.

♦ We can be confident that our Bible today is faithful to the original manuscripts, despite differences that exist in ancient copies.

GOSPEL	DATE (APPROXIMATE)	SOURCE
MARK	AD 65	Peter, written by Mark
MATTHEW	AD 75	Matthew
LUKE	AD 75	Luke, a companion of Paul
JOHN	AD 90	John

How Were the Stories Passed Down?

■ What the skeptics claim:

"[The Gospels] were written thirty-five to sixty-five years after Jesus' death, . . . not by people who were eyewitnesses, but by people living later."[2]

(Courtesy of CSNTM.org)

■ What history actually tells us:

In ancient epistles, the author's name appeared at the beginning of the letter, as in this copy of Paul's letter to the Romans. In ancient historical writings—such as the Gospels—the author's name was sometimes omitted.

Yes and no. While it's true that the Gospels were probably written between thirty-five and sixty-five years after the death of Jesus, historical evidence strongly suggests that the sources of the New Testament Gospels were eyewitnesses of the events of Jesus' life. Mark's Gospel emerged around AD 65; the Gospels According to Matthew and Luke began to circulate a decade or so later. John's Gospel seems to have been penned around AD 90. Even with these dates, it is at least *possible* that the sources of these books were eyewitnesses of Jesus. The emergence of Mark's Gospel only thirty years or so after Jesus' death makes it unreasonable to deny that the Gospels, at the very least, *could* have been written by eyewitnesses.[3]

What matters most, though, isn't *when* the Gospels were written. *What matters most is whether the Gospels accurately represent eyewitness accounts of the life and ministry of Jesus.* According to ancient recollections from such early Christian leaders as Papias of Hierapolis, Polycarp of Smyrna, and Irenaeus of Lyons, each of the four New Testament Gospels represents eyewitness testimony about Jesus Christ. According to these recollections—recollections that bear every mark of originating in the first century AD—

- The anecdotes recorded in the Gospel According to Mark are the testimony of Peter, preserved in written form by his translator Mark.

- Luke's Gospel integrates written and oral sources gathered from eyewitnesses by Paul's personal physician, Luke.

- The materials that are unique to the Gospel According to Matthew came from Matthew, a tax collector who deserted a profitable profession to follow Jesus.

- The accounts in the Gospel According to John find their source in the apostle John.[4]

■ What the skeptics claim:

"Stories based on eyewitness accounts are not necessarily reliable, and the same is true a hundredfold for accounts that . . . have been in oral circulation long after the fact."[5]

■ What history actually tells us:

In a culture that passed on information orally — such as the biblical world — it was possible for oral histories to remain reliable for remarkably long periods of time. People in today's world — surrounded by high levels of literacy and easy access to writing materials — are accustomed to recording important information in *written form*. But, especially among the ancient Jews, important teachings were told and retold in rhythmic, repetitive patterns so that students could memorize key truths.[6] These teachings were known as *oral histories*. In these forms, it was possible for teachings and accounts of historical events to remain amazingly consistent from one generation to the next.[7] Much of the Old Testament and some portions of the New Testament — for example, the eyewitness accounts mentioned in Luke 1:2 — may have been passed down as reliable oral histories before they were written.

■ What the skeptics claim:

Stories in the New Testament "were changed with what would strike us today as reckless abandon. They were modified, amplified, and embellished. And sometimes they were made up."[8]

■ What history actually tells us:

The New Testament accounts of Jesus were not made up or changed with "reckless abandon." Consistent oral histories about the life of Jesus and the early church emerged among eyewitnesses shortly after the events occurred; these oral histories remained consistent as they spread across the Roman Empire.

As an example, let's take a look at one of these segments of oral history, recorded in written form in 1 Corinthians 15:3-7.[9] How do we know that these words from the apostle Paul represent part of the oral tradition about Jesus? Paul introduced this summation with two Greek words — *paradidomi* ("handed over" or "delivered") and *paralambano* ("received") — that indicated it was oral tradition. Ancient readers understood these two words, when used together, to imply that the writer was citing oral history.[10]

A quick examination of these verses demonstrates how quickly oral histories emerged among the eyewitnesses of Jesus

The word "canon" comes from the Greek word *kanon*, which meant "measuring stick." In the fourth century AD, the writings that Christians accepted as authoritative began to be known as a "canon" because these witnesses measured the church's faithfulness to Jesus Christ. Christians embraced the Jewish canon—the books known to us as "the Old Testament"—because they believed that the God of the Jewish Scriptures was also the Father of Jesus Christ. Each writing in the New Testament was expected to be connected to an eyewitness of the risen Lord, to be recognized in churches throughout the known world, and not to contradict other writings about Jesus.

This painting from the ruins of Pompeii shows how widely wax tablets and styluses were used to record thoughts in written form.

and how consistent these traditions remained. Even though Paul wrote in Greek, he called the apostle Peter by his Aramaic name, "Cephas." Then, there's the repeated phrase "and that." The phrase rendered "and that" is the Greek translation of an Aramaic method for joining clauses.[11] Based on the grammatical patterns in these verses, it's clear that this oral history originally circulated in Aramaic. And where did people speak Aramaic? In Galilee and Judea, the places where Jesus walked and talked, died and rose from the dead! And when could Paul have received an oral history of the death and resurrection of Jesus in Aramaic? The point at which Paul seems to have learned this version of the historical account was around AD 35 when he visited Jerusalem and heard the story of Jesus from an eyewitness (Galatians 1:18). For Paul to have received a consistent oral history in Aramaic at this time, scholars estimate that this account—a tradition that clearly affirms the essential facts of Jesus' resurrection—first surfaced near Jerusalem shortly after Jesus was crucified.[12]

From this bit of oral history, it's clear that the earliest Christians did *not* recklessly alter their traditions. Otherwise, how could Paul—writing three years after he first visited Corinth—have said to the Corinthians immediately before he quoted this oral history, "I am reminding you, brothers, about the good proclamation that I proclaimed to you," suggesting that Paul proclaimed similar words in each place that he visited? (1 Corinthians 15:1). Clearly, this example from the oral accounts of Jesus' life was *not* "made up" long after the events or "changed with . . . reckless abandon," as the skeptics claim. To the contrary, this oral tradition about Jesus emerged soon after his resurrection and remained relatively unchanged as it spread across the Roman Empire.

(Courtesy of the Schøyen Collection, Oslo and London)

This summary from a medical manual, copied shortly before the time of Jesus, demonstrates some level of literacy among first-century physicians such as Luke.

■ What the skeptics claim:

"There is not a sentence concerning Jesus in the entire New Testament composed by anyone who had ever met the unwilling King of the Jews."[13] "Jesus' own followers . . . were mainly lower-class peasants—fishermen and artisans, for example—and . . . they spoke Aramaic rather than Greek. . . . In the end, it seems unlikely that the uneducated, lower-class, illiterate disciples of Jesus played the decisive role in the literary compositions that have come down through history under their names."[14]

■ What history actually tells us:

Not all of Jesus' first followers were illiterate; even if some followers *were* illiterate, professional scribes—people who were capable of turning oral histories into polished Greek—were readily available even to working-class persons.

In the book that bears the name "Matthew," the apostle Matthew is presented as a tax collector (Matthew 10:3). It's unlikely that any early Christian would have fabricated this bit of vocational trivia. Since Roman governors expected tax collectors to stockpile personal wealth by cheating people, tax collectors rarely made it to the top of anyone's list of most-loved citizens. But there was one skill that tax collectors *did* possess. *They could read and write.* Tax collectors carried *pinakes*, hinged wooden tablets with beeswax coating on each panel.[15] Tax collectors etched notes in the wax using styluses; these notes could be translated later and rewritten on papyrus.[16] Papyri from Egypt prove that tax collectors also wrote receipts for citizens in their villages.[17] So, a tax collector such as Matthew could *not* have been illiterate. The daily tasks of a Galilean tax collector required him to copy and record information in multiple languages.

What about another character whose name is ascribed to a Gospel, the companion of Paul named "Luke"? Compared to other people in the New Testament, Luke is a quite obscure character. He's mentioned only three times in letters attributed to Paul (Colossians 4:14; Philemon 1:24; 2 Timothy 4:11). Considering how many of Paul's partners enjoy far greater prominence in the New Testament—Timothy, for example, or Barnabas or Silas—it's difficult to explain why anyone would ascribe the third Gospel to Luke...unless, of course, Luke actually *was* responsible for the book that bears his name.

According to Colossians 4:14, Luke was Paul's "beloved physician." Ancient physicians seem to have possessed, at least, the capacity to read the summaries of medical knowledge that flourished in the first century. Papyri from Egypt prove that many physicians also wrote reports for law-enforcement officials regarding suspicious injuries, as well as statements for slave-masters certifying the health of slaves.[18] So, it's unlikely that Luke was completely "illiterate." What's more, many physicians could pull together various eyewitness accounts into coherent reports, just as the preface of Luke's Gospel suggests that the author has done (Luke 1:1-4).

(Courtesy of CSNTM.org)

John Rylands Papyrus 52 records portions of John 18. The writing style and material suggest that this fragment was copied around AD 110.

That leaves Mark and John. Though it is by no means certain, these men *may* have been illiterate. Still, in the first century AD, professional scribes were readily available to render messages from other languages, including Aramaic, into polished Greek. Complex legal titles, epistles to family members, and simple commercial receipts all required secretarial skills—and provided livelihoods for a multitude of scribes.[19] Even though Paul was completely capable of writing in Greek (Galatians 6:11; Philemon 1:19-21), scribes penned Paul's letters for him (Romans 16:22; see also 1 Peter 5:12).[20] It's entirely possible that Mark and John employed professional scribes to render their oral accounts of Jesus' life into Greek documents. If so, they would still have been the *sources* of these Gospels.[21]

How Can We Know that the Bible was Copied Accurately?

■ What the skeptics claim:

"The [Old Testament] is filled with lots of textual problems—as we have come to realize, for example, with the discovery of the Dead Sea Scrolls."[22]

■ What history actually tells us:

In truth, the Dead Sea Scrolls proved the precise opposite. The Dead Sea Scrolls demonstrated how carefully the Old Testament had been copied through the centuries. Around AD 900—nearly a millennium after the time of Jesus—groups of Jewish scribes known as Masoretes began to copy the Old Testament texts according to strict guidelines. The Masoretes maintained nearly perfect accuracy in their copies. Until the discovery of the Dead Sea Scrolls, these Masoretic texts were the oldest available manuscripts of the Old Testament. When the Dead Sea Scrolls were unearthed in the mid-twentieth century, scholars compared the text of Isaiah from the Dead Sea Scrolls with the text of Isaiah preserved by the Masoretes. What these scholars discovered was that—even though more than 1,000 years separated the Dead Sea Scrolls from the Masoretic texts—the Dead Sea Scrolls and the Masoretic texts agreed word-for-word more than 95% of the time![23] The remaining differences stemmed primarily from minor spelling variations. Even the scrolls that differ a bit more than the Isaiah scrolls—for example, the copies of 1 and 2 Samuel and Deuteronomy—do not differ in any way that affects any crucial Jewish or Christian belief.

> *Sir Frederic Kenyon,* former director of the British Museum, commented concerning the Gospels, "The interval between the dates of the original composition and the earliest extant evidence [is] so small as to be negligible, and the last foundation for any doubt that the Scriptures have come down to us substantially as they were written has now been removed."[37]

■ What the skeptics claim:

"There are more differences among our manuscripts than there are words in the New Testament.... We have only error-ridden copies, and the vast majority of these are centuries removed from the originals and different from them...in thousands of ways."[24]

■ What history actually tells us:

More than ninety-nine percent of the variants in the New Testament are not even noticeable when the text is translated; of the remaining differences, *none* affects any vital aspect of Christian faith.[25]

Scholars have 5,700 or so ancient biblical manuscripts available to them. Although many of these manuscripts include the entire New Testament, most are partial copies, found in fragmented form in the sands of Egypt or in the monasteries of Europe and western Asia. All totaled, these manuscripts include more than two million pages of text. In these two-million-plus pages of biblical text, there are between 200,000 and 400,000 variations in wording or spelling. In a complete Greek New Testament, there are approximately 138,000 words. So, yes, there *are* more differences among the total manuscripts than there are words in one complete Greek New Testament. What the skeptics don't clearly communicate to their readers, though, is *the sheer insignificance of these variants.*

(Courtesy of the Schøyen Collection, Oslo and London)

Most of these 400,000 variations stem from differences in spelling, word order, or the relationships between nouns and definite articles—slight variants that are easily recognizable. After minor spelling errors and slight variations in word order are factored out, there is more than 99% agreement between all of the known manuscripts of the Bible! Of the remaining variants, none affects any crucial element of the Christian faith.

■ What the skeptics claim:

"Scribes who were not altogether satisfied with what the New Testament books said modified their words to make them ... more vigorously oppose heretics, women, Jews, and pagans."[26]

■ What history actually tells us:

With more than 5,700 manuscripts and fragments of the New Testament available to us, it would be impossible for anyone to have modified major portions the New Testament without their changes being quite easily noticed. In the few cases when changes *were* attempted, the original text can—in all but the tiniest handful of instances—be easily restored by examining the most ancient New Testament manuscripts.[27]

Some scribes after the New Testament era may have altered texts that placed women in prominent positions. For example, in Romans 16:7, someone named Junia—a name that appears to be feminine—is said to be "significant among the apostles," but a later scribe seems to have turned "Junia" into "Junias," a man's name.[28] In the most ancient manuscripts of Acts 18:26, a woman named Priscilla is the primary teacher of Apollos. Centuries later, a copyist switched the order of names, placing the name of Priscilla's husband first. These kinds of changes are, however, obvious and easy to identify.

WORKS OF PLATO	NEW TESTAMENT
• Written around 400 BC • Only seven copies have survived • The earliest surviving manuscript was copied between AD 800 and 900 — more than 1,200 years after the original documents were written	• Written between AD 60 and 100 • More than 5,700 portions have survived • Complete manuscripts of the New Testament have survived from the late third or early fourth centuries — less than three centuries after the original documents were written • Hundreds of fragments and manuscripts have survived from the second, third, and fourth centuries

Even in the very few cases that remain uncertain, the problem is not with the texts themselves. The difficulty is with the choices of individuals to twist biblical texts to sanction negative attitudes toward women, Jews, or non-believers. In any case, the claim that the Bible as we have it today has been modified for the purpose of opposing women, Jews, and pagans has no substantive foundation in the actual texts.

■ What the skeptics claim:

"Many of our cherished biblical stories and widely held beliefs concerning the divinity of Jesus, the Trinity, and the divine origins of the Bible itself stem from both intentional and accidental alterations by scribes."[29]

TIME LINE

AD50

28–30: Approximate dates of Jesus' earthly ministry, beginning in the fifteenth year of Caesar Tiberius (Luke 3:1).

57–62: Paul arrested in Jerusalem, spent two years in Roman custody before appealing to Caesar (Acts 21–28).

33: Paul saw Jesus on the road to Damascus (Acts 9).

47–49: Paul went to Asia Minor on his first missionary journey. In AD 49, Caesar Claudius expelled all Jews from Rome — according to Roman historian Suetonius — because of riots "on account of a certain Chrestus," probably a reference to Jesus Christ (Acts 13–15).

■ **What history actually tells us:**

This claim is simply not true. Firm belief in the divinity of the Jesus, the threefold nature of God, and the divine origins of the Bible emerged among Christians before the New Testament was even completed. None of these beliefs depends on disputed or altered passages in the Bible. It is true that one verse that mentions the Trinity was not originally present in the biblical text: The last half of 1 John 5:7—a text that, in some later manuscripts, reads, "There are three that testify in heaven, the Father, the Word, and the Spirit, and these three are one"—doesn't appear in the most ancient New Testament manuscripts. But the doctrine of the Trinity does not depend on this verse. God's nature as three-yet-one is affirmed just as clearly in Matthew 28:19, where Jesus commanded his followers to baptize in the *name* (singular) of the Father, Son, and Spirit. Similarly, the most ancient copies of 1 Timothy 3:16 declare, "Great is the mystery of godliness; he was manifested in the flesh," while a few later texts read, "*God* was manifested in the flesh." But, again, the doctrine of the deity of Jesus does *not* depend on this text; the deity of Jesus is clearly affirmed in several undisputed texts, including John 20:28, where Thomas recognized Jesus as Lord and God. No essential Christian belief is affected by any variant in the biblical manuscripts.

Who Chose the Books in My Bible?

■ **What the skeptics claim:**

"Many Christians today may think that the canon of the New Testament simply appeared on the scene one day, soon after the death of Jesus, but nothing could be farther from the truth. As it turns out, we are able to pinpoint the first time that any Christian of record listed the twenty-seven books of our New Testament as *the* books of the New Testament— neither more nor fewer. . . . In the year 367, Athanasius wrote his annual pastoral letter to the Egyptian churches under his jurisdiction, and in it he . . . lists our twenty-seven books, excluding all others."[30]

TIME LINE

AD100

c. 35–c. 117: Ignatius of Antioch was a disciple of John, the author of the Gospel; he wrote seven letters to churches as he traveled to Rome to suffer martyrdom during the reign of Emperor Trajan. In these letters, he quoted sayings that are found in Gospels of Matthew and Luke as well as Acts, Romans, 1 Corinthians, Ephesians, Colossians, and 1 Thessalonians.[36] These quotations demonstrate that early Christians treated these texts as authoritative. ·········

66–70: After years of enduring oppression from Roman governors, the Jews revolted. Their rebellion resulted in the destruction of the Jewish temple in AD 70.

■ What history actually tells us:

This statement leaves out several key facts about the selection of the New Testament books. It is true that Athanasius was the first author to list the exact same twenty-seven books that we find in the New Testament today. Yet, from the beginning, Christians unanimously accepted the four Gospels, Acts, Paul's letters, and the first epistle of John. Although disputes about a few New Testament books lasted into the fourth century, widespread agreement about which writings were authoritative existed among Christians from the first century onward. The primary standard for deciding which books were authoritative emerged long before the fourth century—and the standard *wasn't* the word of a powerful bishop. Hints of this standard can, in fact, be found in Christian writings of the first century AD. The basic idea was this: *Testimony that could be connected to eyewitnesses of the risen Lord was uniquely authoritative among early Christians.*[31] From the beginning, authoritative testimony about Jesus Christ had to have its source in eyewitnesses of the risen Lord. Even while the New Testament books were being written, the words of people who saw and followed the risen Lord carried special weight in the churches (see Acts 1:21-26; 15:6 — 16:5; 1 Corinthians 4 — 5; 9:1-12; Galatians

1:1-12; 1 Thessalonians 5:26-27). The logic of this standard was simple: The people most likely to know the truth about Jesus were eyewitnesses who had encountered Jesus personally or their close associates.

(Courtesy of the Schøyen Collection, Oslo and London)
The sermons of the third-century theologian Origen of Alexandria clearly recognized the authority of the New Testament writings.

Although debates continued into the fourth century about a few writings—including the letters of Peter, John's second and third letters, and the letters of James and Jude—Christians universally agreed at least as early as the second century on the authority of no fewer than nineteen of the books in the New Testament—and these are the writings that reflect some of the most essential truths about Jesus. Even if this score or so of books had been the only documents that represented eyewitness testimony about Jesus, every vital truth of Christian faith would remain completely intact. What directed this process was the conviction that these writings must be rooted in reliable, eyewitness testimony about Jesus Christ.

TIME LINE

AD150

c. 69–c. 155: Polycarp of Smyrna was a disciple of John, the author of the Gospel. In 155 or 156, Polycarp suffered martyrdom for his faith.

c. 60–c. 135: Papias of Hierapolis was a disciple of John, the author of the Gospel; Papias recorded several ancient traditions about the origins of the Gospels.

When deciding which Old Testament writings to accept, Christians embraced the same listing of books as the Jewish people. When the Septuagint—a popular Greek-language version of the Jewish holy writings—was translated around 200 BC, the translators had included some Jewish writings which never appeared in the Hebrew Scriptures and which Jewish rabbis rejected around AD 90 at the Council of Jamnia (Yavneh). The Roman Catholic and Eastern Orthodox Churches recognize these additional books from the Septuagint as authoritative; these writings appear in the Roman Catholic and Eastern Orthodox Bibles as "deuterocanonical" or "apocryphal" books.

■ What the skeptics claim:

Among the earliest Christians, "there was no agreed-upon canon—and no agreed-upon theology. Instead, there was a wide range of diversity: diverse groups asserting diverse theologies based on diverse written texts, all claiming to be written by apostles of Jesus."[52]

■ What history actually tells us:

Among the people who walked and talked with Jesus, a consensus emerged very early regarding both the identity of Jesus and all but a few biblical books. It's true that there *were* several divergent sets of beliefs that circulated within the earliest churches. It's also true that debates about a few biblical books lasted beyond the first and second centuries. Yet the persons who actually walked and talked with Jesus agreed about the nature of Jesus even before the New Testament was completed. Consensus about all but a few New Testament books was reached by the mid-second century, probably earlier. According to the records found in the New Testament—the only writings about Jesus that were written early enough to be connected to eyewitnesses of Jesus—Jesus was human and yet divine, he was the messianic king predicted in the Hebrew Scriptures, he was physically raised from the dead, and it is only by trusting in him that anyone can enjoy the life that God created humanity to live, both now and in eternity (see Jn. 20:28-31; 1 Cor. 15:1-7; 1 Jn. 2:22; 4:1-3). According to the eyewitnesses of Jesus, to deny such truths as these was to exclude oneself from fellowship with Jesus Christ and with his followers (see 1 Jn. 4:1-6).

TIME LINE

AD200

........130–202: Irenaeus of Lyons repeated the same traditions that Papias reported nearly a century earlier, adding, "The heretics boast that they have many more gospels than there really are. ... But there are only four authentic gospels. These alone were written by Jesus' true followers."

(Courtesy of CSNTM.org)

This painting of the apostle John appears at the beginning of John's Gospel in a thirteenth-century manuscript.

How Reliable is My Bible?

■ What the skeptics claim:

"Not only do we not have the originals [of the biblical manuscripts], we don't have the first copies of the originals.... What we have are copies made later — much later."[33]

■ What history actually tells us:

Although the original manuscripts from the biblical authors *have* been lost–probably forever–the copies that we possess today reliably reflect the inspired message of the original authors. Ancient people saw no reason to revere original manuscripts from important people, and–once documents became too worn to read easily–they did not retain the original manuscripts.[34] Instead, they made reliable copies and burned or buried the originals. Occasionally, the ink was scraped from the original, and the parchment was reused.

Despite the critics' claims, it *is* possible that we possess first-generation copies of the original New Testament manuscripts. In AD 200, churches in Corinth, Philippi, Thessalonica, Ephesus, and Rome still possessed original manuscripts from the apostolic authors.[35] Many portions of the New Testament that were copied between AD 100 and 200 have been found in Egypt; it is entirely possible that scribes copied at least a few of these documents from the original manuscripts.

What matters most, however, is not the *age* of the existing manuscripts but their *reliability*. When the manuscripts are compared, they completely agree with one another more than 99% of the time. Of the differences that remain, *not even one difference* decisively affects any aspect of Christian faith.

A Final Word

So will there be more sensational new findings about the Gospels—findings that supposedly demonstrate that these writings don't contain the gospel truth after all? Of course! The Holy Bible has withstood thousands of attempts to destroy its truth and to discredit its authority, and yet no one has succeeded. The truth and the authority of the Scriptures stand strong, regardless of every attempt to render them ineffective. So can the Bible be trusted? In a word, *yes*.

Author: Timothy Paul Jones, Ed.D
Excerpted material © 2007 Dr. Timothy Paul Jones. Excerpted from the book *Misquoting Truth: A Guide to the Fallacies of Bart Ehrman's Misquoting Jesus.* Published by InterVarsity Press (www.ivpress.com). All rights reserved. Reprinted by permission.
Visit the author on the Internet at: www.TimothyPaulJones.com
Special thanks to Alfred J. Hoerth, Director of Archaeology, Emeritus, Wheaton College; Lew Whallon.

Endnotes

1   Representative selections from Bart Ehrman, *Misquoting Jesus: The Story Behind Who Changed the Bible and Why* (New York: HarperCollins, 2005) 7, 10-11, 57. Hereafter, *Misquoting Jesus* will be cited as *MJ*, followed by the page numbers.

2   Bart Ehrman, *Jesus, Apocalyptic Prophet of the New Millennium* (New York: Oxford University, 1999) *JApP* 44-45. Hereafter, *Jesus, Apocalyptic Prophet of the New Millennium* will be cited as *JApP*, followed by the page numbers.

3   R. Bauckham, *Jesus and the Eyewitnesses: The Gospels as Eyewitness Testimony* (Grand Rapids, MI: William B. Eerdmans, 2006) 8-9, 20, 252-289.

4   Eusebius of Caesarea, *Historia Ecclesiastica*, 3:39; 5:8, 20; Bauckham, 14, 295-296; M. Hengel, *The Four Gospels and the One Gospel of Jesus Christ*, trans. John Bowden (Harrisburg, PA: Trinity Press, 2000) 36; C.-J. Thornton, *Der Zeuge des Zeugen: Lukas als Historiker der Paulusreisen*, ed. M. Hengel *WUNT* 56 (Tubingen, Germany: J.C.B. Mohr/Paul Siebeck, 1991) 10-82.

5   *JApP* 47-52.

6   For survey of orality in rabbinic and early Christian practice, see A. Millard, *Reading and Writing in the Time of Jesus* (New York: New York University Press, 2000), 188-192; R. Stein, *The Method and Message of Jesus' Teachings* rev. ed. (Louisville, KY: Westminster John Knox, 1994) 27-32; J. Harvey, *Listening to the Text: Oral Patterning in Paul's Letters* (Grand Rapids: Baker, 1998).

7   J.D.G. Dunn, *Jesus Remembered* (Grand Rapids, MI: William B. Eerdmans, 2003) 192-254; B. Witherington III, *The Jesus Quest* (Downers Grove, IL: InterVarsity Press, 1995) 80; see also
J. Vansina, *Oral Tradition as History* (Madison, WI: University of Wisconsin, 1985) 15, 190-195.

8   Bart Ehrman, *Peter, Paul, and Mary Magdalene: The Followers of Jesus in History and Legend* (New York: Oxford University, 2006) 259. Hereafter, *Peter, Paul, and Mary Magdalene: The Followers of Jesus in History and Legend* will be cited as *PPM*, followed by the page numbers.

9   K. MacGregor, "1 Corinthians 15:3b—6a, 7 and the Bodily Resurrection of Jesus," in *Journal of the Evangelical Theological Society* 49 (June 2006): 225-234.

10   N.T. Wright, *The Resurrection of the Son of God* (Philadelphia, PA: Fortress, 2003) 318-319.

11   The repeated word-pattern which "and that" apparently translates is the distinctly Semitic *vav* consecutive. See P. Lapide, *The Resurrection of Jesus: A Jewish Perspective* (Minneapolis, MN: Augsburg, 1983) 98-99; G. Fee, *The First Epistle to the Corinthians* (Grand Rapids, MI: Eerdmans, 1987); 719, 722-726.

12   G. Ludemann, *The Resurrection of Jesus* (London, UK: SCM, 1994) 38; R. Funk, et al., *The Acts of Jesus* (San Francisco, CA: Polebridge, 1998) 454.

13   H. Bloom, *Jesus and Yahweh* (New York: Riverhead, 2005) 19.

14   *JApP* 45.

15   Millard, 28-29. Some scholars have argued that the apostles were literate and that they would have carried *pinakes* and noted significant sayings of Jesus. It seems to me, however, that this assumes a higher rate of literacy in Galilee and Judea—especially among persons in trades such as fishing—than the available evidence can sustain. For discussion and references, see B. Gerhardsson, *The Origins of the Gospel Traditions* (London, UK: SCM, 1979) 68-161, and, S. Lieberman, *Hellenism in Jewish Palestine* (New York: JTS, 1962) 203.

16   The abundance of surviving Roman taxation receipts, written in Greek, clearly demonstrates this fact. The epigraphical evidence includes not only brief receipts that follow simple formulas—for examples, see the numerous pieces of Elephantine and Egyptian ostraca in U. Wilken, *Griechische Ostraka aus Aegypten und Nubien* (Manchester, NH: Ayer, 1979) and in F. Preisigke, et al., *Sammelbuch griechischer Urkunden aus Aegypten* (Berlin: Walter de Gruyter, 1974)—but also more lengthy and complex receipts on papyrus, such as *POxy* 51:3609.

17   Millard, 31, 170. See the taxation documentation from the pre-Christian era and from the first and second centuries AD found in the Oxyrhynchus papyri *POxy* 49:3461; *POxy* 62:4334; *POxy* 24:2413; *POxy* 45:3241; and, *POxy* 66:4527, as well as more extensive contractual agreements such as the third-century *POxy* 43:3092.

18   J. Huskinson, *Experiencing Rome: Culture, Identity, and Power in the*

Roman Empire (London, UK: Routledge, 2000) 179-180; Nutton, 263-264. For a few of the many documentary examples of literacy among ancient physicians, see *P.Mich* 758; *POxy* 44:3195; *POxy* 45:3245; *POxy* 54:3729; *POxy* 63:4366; *POxy* 63:4370; *POxy* 64:4441; *POxy* 66:4529.

19   Millard, 176-185; R. Cribbiore, *Writing, Teachers, and Students in Graeco-Roman Egypt* (Atlanta, GA: Scholars, 1996) 1-5.

20   Ehrman seems to view the fact that a scribe wrote on Paul's behalf as being problematic for persons who embrace the Bible as divine truth (*MJ* 59), but Paul's use of a scribe does not preclude Paul's position as the source of the epistle. Certainly, he would have approved the letter before it was sent.

21   It is crucial to note that ancient persons were considered to be the writers of a document, even if they used a scribe to write the words. Notice how Paul declared, "I have written to you" in Romans 15:15, even though Tertius penned the actual document (see Romans 16:22). In the oral culture of the ancient Roman Empire, what scribes apparently recorded was the speaker-writer's oral performance of the document. This performance was then "re-performed" by the courier of the document. See J. Small, *Wax Tablets of the Mind: Cognitive Studies of Memory and Literacy in Classical Antiquity* (New York: Routledge, 1997) 160-201; Gregory Snyder, *Teachers and Texts in the Ancient World: Philosophers, Jews and Christians* (London, UK: Routledge, 2000) 191, 226-227; R. Thomas, *Literacy and Orality in Ancient Greece* (Cambridge, UK: Cambridge University Press, 2002) 36-40, 124-125.

22   Bart Ehrman, *Misquoting Jesus* expanded paperback edition (New York: HarperSanFrancisco, 2007) 254.

23   Gleason Archer, *A Survey of Old Testament Introduction* (Chicago, IL: Moody Press, 1994) 29.

24   *MJ* 7, 10-11.

25   D. Wallace, "The Gospel According to Bart," in *Journal of the Evangelical Theological Society* 49 (June 2006): 330.

26   *MJ* 149.

27   Bruce Metzger and Bart Ehrman, *The Text of the New Testament: Its Transmission, Corruption, and Restoration* (New York: Oxford University Press, 2005), 288-290.

28   Though I agree with Ehrman that "Junia" was a woman, the case is—in all fairness—not quite as clear-cut as Ehrman presents it. For an alternative viewpoint, see D. Wallace, "Junia among the Apostles": Retrieved December 1, 2006, from http://www.bible.org/page.php?page_id=1163/.

29   *MJ* dust jacket.

30   Bart Ehrman, *Lost Christianities* (New York: Oxford University Press, 2003) 54, 230.

31   Ehrman places the emergence of this principle later and summarizes it in this way: Authoritative texts had to be "ancient" (from the time of Jesus) and "apostolic" (from the first followers of Jesus or their associates) (*LC* 242-243). As Ehrman notes, two other standards came into play later in addition to antiquity and apostolicity; these two additional standards were *catholicity* (widespread usage among Christians) and *orthodoxy* (agreement with other Scriptures). For the earliest Christians, the three categories of *orthodoxy*, *apostolicity*, and *antiquity* do not seem to have been distinguished; all three categories were rooted in the assumption that eyewitness testimony was authoritative.

32   *MJ* 153.

33   *MJ* 7, 11.

34   Millard, 20, 33-34.

35   "Age iam, qui uoles curiositatem melius exercere in negotio salutis tuae, percurre ecclesias apostolicas apud quas ipsae adhuc cathedrae apostolorum suis locis praesident, apud quas ipsae *authenticae litterae* eorum recitantur sonantes uocem et repraesentantes faciem uniuscuiusque" (Tertullian of Carthage, *De Praescriptione Haereticorum*, 36:1: Retrieved November 4, 2006, from http://www.tertullian.org/).

36   *To the Ephesians* 10:2; 14:2; 18:1; 20:2; *To the Magnesians* 5:1; *To the Trallians* 1:3; 12:3; *To the Romans* 5:1-2; 6:1; *To the Smyrnans* 3:1-2; 6:1; *To Polycarp* 1:2; 2:2; 5:1.

37   F.F. Bruce, *The New Testament Documents: Are they Reliable?* (Downers Grove, IL: Inter Varsity, 1972) 20.

Myths about Heaven

Myth: Heaven will be boring.

Myth: We will be disembodied spirits in heaven.

Myth: We will lose our identity in heaven.

Myth: All people go to heaven.

Why is heaven important?

Heaven is more than just hope for a better future. It is at the heart of God's plan for all creation. It is also at the center of the human heart.

The common experience of losing loved ones, and the eventual loss of our own lives, make the issue of heaven one with which everyone must wrestle. We wonder what happens when we die, when our loved ones die. Have we lost them forever? Are they in a better place? Will we see them again someday? What is life after death like? What is heaven like? Can we even know something about heaven?

Heaven is a source of hope, guidance, and meaning for every believer. Heaven gives:

- Hope for our future destination and strength for life in the present
- Guidance for living as God's people today
- Meaning by giving us the certainty that there is more to life than this world

In the following pages, we will explore some of the most common questions and popular myths about heaven. We will also broaden our perspective about heaven. We will realize that heaven is not only about *hope* but also about *faith* and *love*.

© PHOTOCREO Michal Sedláček

What do we mean by heaven?

In popular culture, and for many believers, heaven evokes images of cloudy, ghost-like existence, or angelic beings floating about among the clouds. This image comes directly from the radical separation of the physical and spiritual worlds. Some of the misconceptions are:

Popular View of Heaven
- A place for disembodied, ghost-like beings
- A place where people sing all the time
- A place up by the clouds
- A place everyone goes after death
- A place where all beings live as angels

Biblical View of Heaven
However, the final destination of believers is not an ethereal place like that. The final destination of all believers is *the renewed heavens and earth* anticipated in Revelation 21. A very physical, concrete future awaits us when Christ comes back.

What can we know about heaven?

The answer is not as much as we would like; however, we can know just enough to be confident that:

- We can trust in God's promises.
- We will be with God and our loved ones.
- God will do something awesome with his creation.

How do we know anything about heaven?

- The only completely valid source of knowledge about heaven is the Bible. The Bible has direct and indirect information about heaven—over 600 verses in the Bible mention *heaven*.
- The Bible is the rule with which we can decide if other information is valid.
- However, for the most part, people's ideas about heaven come mainly from literature, movies, and television. Media has shaped much of our imagination and knowledge about heaven. Not all of this knowledge is accurate.
- A non-biblical understanding of the world has informed much of what popular culture knows about heaven.
- It mainly portrays heaven as boring and unappealing.

A non-biblical understanding of the universe

Behind the cloudy, ethereal idea of heaven lies the old Gnostic belief that the physical world is evil and the spiritual is good. Thus, one must focus on the spiritual to escape this evil world. This is not a biblical idea. It ignores some basic biblical facts:

A biblical understanding of the universe

1. God made the whole universe and called it *very good* (Gen. 1:31).

2. Satan is a spiritual being and is evil—thus, not all *spiritual* is good and not all *physical* is evil.

3. God promises a renewed heavens and earth at the end of time (Rev. 21).

Although sin has profoundly affected creation, God never called creation evil. It is under a curse. However, Jesus came to lift that curse and turn it into blessing. God is redeeming all of creation. At the end of time, God will renew all things to their original intention.

Understanding God's original plan for his creation helps us understand our final destination as well.

What was God's original intent for creation?

God created the whole universe for his own glory and relationships. He intended all his creatures to relate to each other, to nature, and to himself in harmony. Humanity's main and great goal in life is to glorify God (Isa. 60:21; 1 Cor. 6:20; 10:31) and enjoy him forever (Phil. 4:4; Rev. 21:3–4).

Human sin twisted God's original intentions. However, because of God's grace and faithfulness, his plans would not be frustrated. He planned to rescue his creation from the effects of sin (Rom. 8:18–27). Through the saving work of Jesus on the cross, people can find peace with God and each other. Through the same process, believers can begin the reconciliation with one another and nature.

Neos and Kainos

Greek has two different words for the idea of *new*. *Neos* is a newness of time; *kainos* is a newness of quality. A *neos* object would mean that the object did not exist and now is there. A *kainos* object means that the object was there but its quality has changed: it is better, it is made different. In this sense, the *new heavens and earth* in Rev. 21:1 are not *neos* but *kainos*. That is, God will renew, transform, improve, and refresh his creation. It will be a *kainos* heaven and earth.

What is the renewed heaven and earth?

© Andrejs Pidjass

This process will have a glorious ending when Christ returns. He will renew all things (Rev. 21:1). It will not be a different creation or a non-creation. It will be *this* creation renewed; God will restore his creation to its original glory and purpose. As if to close the circle, what God began at Eden he will fulfill in Revelation. Not everything will be the same. Some things from the biblical idea of Eden will continue in the renewed creation; others will end.

We do have glimpses of heaven, even if many things are not clear. We can see it in the love we experience for and from people, in the majesty of nature's beauty and power, in the generosity and kindness of people in times of need, in the smile of a happy baby, in the loyalty and warmth of our pets, in the tenderness and wisdom of old age, and in moments of deep emotional and spiritual connections with our loved ones and God.

What is our hope for the future?

Our hope for the future is firmly rooted in God's faithfulness. We can trust that God will do what he has promised us because he has been faithful in the past. We can safely conclude that many features and characteristics of this world will continue in the renewed creation. Of course, there will be things that will end as well. Based on biblical testimony, we can identify many things that will continue and some that will not.

© Monkey Business Images

What Will Continue	What Will End

• Physical bodies
• Emotions (relationships)
• Nature
   Daily cycles
   Weather
   Animals—including pets
• Many activities, such as:
   Work (Gen. 2:15)
   Learning (1 Cor. 13:12)
   Science
   Art (Rev. 14:2–3)
   Entertainment
	• No evil
	• No curse
	• No brokenness, emotional or physical
	• No more sin
	• No death
	• No marriage
	• No more suffering or sadness
	• No war
	• No famine
	• No need for temples

"This is the will of Him who sent Me, that of all that He has given Me I lose nothing, but raise it up on the last day." —John 6:39 (*NASB*)

Besides referring to people, this text also refers to God's creation. The neuter pronoun *it* (Greek *auto*) would seem to extend Jesus' mission from people to all of creation (see Romans 8:19–22 and Colossians 1:20). Jesus' words in John 6:29 are a guarantee that no good thing shall be lost, but rather shall have some new and fulfilled form in the renewed creation. Everything good belongs to Christ, who is the life of the whole world as well as the life of every believer (John 6:33, 40). All things good in this world will continue to exist in the next, but they will be transformed and improved in the renewed creation.

Why does Jesus' resurrection matter?

Jesus' resurrection gives us a good idea of what heaven may look like. The Apostle Paul makes it clear that our future is tied to Jesus' own resurrection (1 Cor. 15:12–34). He concludes, "And if Christ has not been raised, your faith is futile…" (15:17).

- Because Christ has been raised from the dead, our hope is true and secured.
- Christ is the firstfruits or first example of all who will be raised into new life (15:20).
- Our future includes a *resurrected body*; that is, it will be a physical reality. Our future resurrected bodies will be like Jesus' own resurrected body (1 Cor. 15:42–49).
- The women and the disciples recognized Jesus after his resurrection (Matt. 28:9, 17).
- Jesus' body was physical (Lk. 24:39). Jesus ate with his disciples (Lk. 24:41–43). Yet, it was not a body like ours. The Apostle Paul uses two ways to explain this difference:

1. Just as different animals have bodies suited for their environment (for the sea, the air, and the ground), so our resurrected bodies will be suited for the renewed creation (1 Cor. 15:39).
2. There are also "natural bodies" and "spiritual bodies." Both Jesus' pre- and post-Resurrection bodies were physical; the difference is about perishability. That is, natural bodies die; spiritual bodies do not. Sin has polluted and damaged our natural bodies; our bodies die, decay, and are unfit for a future in God's presence. Just as God will renew this creation, also marred by sin, God will give us renewed bodies that will not be polluted by sin, will not decay, and will be fit to be in the presence of God.

© R. Gino Santa Maria

Natural Bodies	Spiritual Bodies
Psychikos	*Pneumatikos*
Derived from *psyche*, meaning "soul"	Derived from *pneuma*, meaning "spirit"

The ending *ikos* is used in Greek to make an adjective, and it means "in reference to." It does not describe the material out of which something is made. Rather, it refers to the force that animates an object. In this case, *psychikos* refers to the human soul that animates our bodies. In the case of *pneumatikos*, it refers to the Spirit, God's Spirit, as the animating force (see, for example, Rom. 1:11 and Gal. 6:1). Thus, both kinds of bodies are physical. The difference is that a "natural body" dies and a "spiritual body" does not die.

Will we be able to recognize our loved ones in heaven?

Yes! When Jesus rose from the dead and appeared to his friends and disciples, they recognized him (Luke 24:39; John 20:27). There will be continuity between our bodies today and our resurrected bodies in the renewed creation.

© Tiffany Chan

> *I know that my Redeemer lives, and that in the end he will stand upon the earth. And after my skin has been destroyed, yet in my flesh I will see God; I myself will see him with my own eyes—I, and not another. How my heart yearns within me!*
> —Job 19:25–27

© Monkey Business Images

What kinds of relationships will exist in heaven?

Emotions and relationships are a very important part of what it means to be human. There will be emotions and relationships in heaven, though they may not be exactly the same. They will be renewed emotions, emotions as they were meant to be from the beginning: joyful, satisfying, enriching, intimate, and refreshing.

There will be no sorrow, or regrets, or guilt. Rather, love, compassion, gentleness, tenderness, and other emotions will find new heights and depths in heaven. Relationships will be all we can imagine and more.

Will there be disabilities, injuries or deformities in heaven?

No. There will be no brokenness at all, either emotional or physical. God will renew our bodies; they will be beautiful and work as God intended them to. Because Jesus' injuries were present after his resurrection (Luke 24:39; John 20:27), many people think that martyrs, those who died for the name of Jesus, will wear their healed scars as badges of honor. Although it is possible, it remains, like so many other things about heaven, just speculation.

Will we keep our uniqueness in heaven? What about language, food, and clothing?

Because we do not understand the nature of the future bodies, it is difficult to know whether food, clothing, and languages will be necessary or not.
However, since our bodies will preserve much of their uniqueness, we could imagine that language, food, and clothing could be very similar. The beautiful diversity of characters and gifts makes life more interesting. Each person reflects God's image in a way that none other can. Together, with our differences and similarities, with our talents and strengths, we reflect God's image as no individual human could.

Yet, there will certainly be differences as well. Today, differences in language, food, and clothing (cultures, in general) can be causes of deep, fierce divisions (Gen. 11:1–9). However, in the renewed creation, communication will be transparent. We will say what we mean, and people will fully understand us. This side of heaven, clothing can be used as a status symbol that can serve our pride. It is also used to cover our shame. There will be no shame in the renewed creation, nor will we have the need to boost our ego at the expense of others. Rather, clothing will not conceal but could reveal our inner being.

© Monkey Business Images

Will heaven be boring?

Definitely not! People may get the idea that heaven will be boring because we will worship God all day long in heaven. It is true—we will worship God non-stop! But let's revisit what we mean by *worship*.

Worship is not just the singing and praying part of Christian church services. Everything we do can be worship: from the moment we wake up, take our meals, relate to others, do our work, play games, and live life. Worship is not just an activity; it is primarily an attitude. Worship is the attitude that arises when we recognize who God is and who we are:

God	Human
He is the creator	We are the creatures
He is in control of our lives	We depend completely on God's grace and mercy
He is all powerful	We are limited and weak
He knows all things	We know imperfectly
He loves us unconditionally	We are just learning to love in the same way

Worship is the attitude that acknowledges God's presence at every moment in our daily lives, sometimes moving us to tears, sometimes to great joy, to repentance, to humility, to gratitude, to hard work, to commitment, to compassion, to love.

In the busyness of our lives, we often miss this reality: God is interested and active in our lives! We may go days or weeks without realizing that our words, actions, and thoughts have brought glory or sadness to God. This forgetfulness will find no place in the renewed creation; we will not miss God in our lives because he will dwell in our midst.

© Donald Linscott

Worship = an attitude of awe and gratitude, of humble submission to God's greatness and grace, of obedience and love.

What will we do in heaven?

The Bible does not give many details about activities in heaven. But we can be sure that:

- God loves his creation. He proclaimed it good (Gen. 1:31).
- Nature itself reflects God's greatness and glory (Ps. 19).
- Nature will be renewed so it may fulfill God's purposes.

So it is at least possible that much of the new creation will be similar to what we experience now. The best things about this world will just become better in the renewed creation.

Will we have pets?

Our relationships with our pets are also important and meaningful. These relationships reflect the way God intended us to relate to animals in general: with love, respect, and companionship. Will God, then, resurrect our beloved pets? Yes, it is perfectly possible. We cannot be sure, since the Bible does not address this issue, but based on God's love for animals, their role as our companions, it is at least possible.

© Quincy Dein

The wolf and the lamb will feed together, and the lion will eat straw like the ox, but dust will be the serpent's food. They will neither harm nor destroy on all my holy mountain.
                    —Isaiah 65:25

Will there be work?

Because work can become an almost painful toil, we often wonder if *rest* means no more working. But remember that

- Work is also a form of worship;

- God meant for humans to help take care of his creation (Gen. 2:15).

Each person will develop and thrive with his or her own talents. We will no longer work in places that do not allow us to grow as individuals, or where our work might be unappreciated, or where we cannot possibly be happy.

God intended work to be a joyful activity. Rather than just making a living, work should be a way to fellowship with God by caring for his world. For this reason, we can be sure we will have plenty of interesting things to do in the renewed creation!

Will there be learning, science, sports, and arts?

As with work, we could imagine the same for learning, science, arts, and sports. The gifts and talents of painters, poets, athletes and scientists will be used simply to worship God.

Whatever you do, work at it with all your heart, as working for the Lord, not for men, since you know that you will receive an inheritance from the Lord as a reward. It is the Lord Christ you are serving.
—Colossians 3:23–24

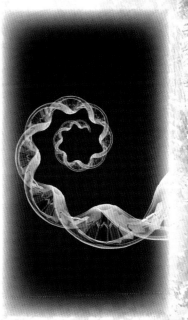

© Lilun

© Motionstream

What's so great about heaven?

Everything! Heaven is all we ever dreamt and more. In this life, we grow, reach our peak, and begin a slow descent until our life ends. Life in the intermediate heaven will be much better because we will be in God's presence. However, life in the renewed creation will be beyond our imagination.

It is true that we do not know many facts about the renewed creation, heaven, and even less about the intermediate state, intermediate heaven. However, what we read in the Bible and what we know about God give us great hope and joy.

> *Dear friends, now we are children of God, and what we will be has not yet been made known. But we know that when he appears, we shall be like him, for we shall see him as he is. Everyone who has this hope in him purifies himself, just as he is pure.*
> —1 John 3:2–3

The Ultimate Great Escape?

- Heaven is not an escapist idea.
- We do not think about heaven to escape this world's troubles—we think about heaven as a guide to live better in this world, to serve God with greater joy, and to show others God's great love.
- For many believers who suffer persecution for their faithfulness, and others who suffer in this life in indescribable ways, heaven is a great source of comfort.

- Knowing that God will make all things right one day gives us strength to continue life in faithfulness and obedience.

Who will be in heaven and how do we get there?

- In popular culture, it's common to believe that all people go to heaven, and, in some cases, they become angels. However, biblical testimony does not support either of these ideas.

- Just as we acknowledge the reality of heaven, we must recognize the reality of hell. We don't know very much about hell either, except that it exists, it is a place of punishment, and there is only one way to escape it. The other details are hidden from us.

- The Bible is clear, however, to specify who will go to heaven. Only those who have surrendered their lives to Jesus and who experience the renewal of their hearts will be allowed in God's presence.

© David Huntley

> *For God so loved the world that he gave his one and only Son, that whoever believes in him shall not perish but have eternal life. For God did not send his Son into the world to condemn the world, but to save the world through him.*
> —John 3:16–17

What is the New Jerusalem?

The book of Revelation provides another image of the renewed creation: the city of Jerusalem (Rev. 21:2). The city is described as a bride and its dimensions are detailed. Believers understand this text in different ways. Some understand the city to be a literal city, and the dimension an accurate representation of what the city will be like. The resulting picture is an enormous cube of about 1,400 miles per side.

Others take this image as a symbolic representation of God's people. Since the image of the bride ready to marry the Lamb occurs before, and it seems applied to God's people (Rev. 19:7), it is possible that the Holy City stands for God's holy people. It is perfectly possible that there will be no seas (21:1), or sun and moon (21:23). It is also possible that the language is symbolic—it says the "city does not need the sun or the moon…" not that they will not exist. If there is continuity between this creation and the renewed creation, as we have suggested, then the beauty of the sun and the moon will be present, even if not needed.

In any case, it is clear that:

- The renewed creation is God's work, since it comes from above.
- It is large enough to fit all of God's people and more.
- It points at the beauty and splendor of the renewed creation.
- God dwells in its midst.
- It closes the circle from Paradise in the Garden of Eden to the Holy City in the new heavens and new earth.

Original Creation (Genesis)	*Renewed Creation (Revelation)*
Heaven and earth created, 1:1	Heavens and earth renewed, 21:1
Sun created, 1:16	No need of sun, 21:23
The night established, 1:5	No night there, 22:5
The seas created, 1:10	No more seas, 21:1
The curse enters the world, 3:14–17	No more curse, 22:3
Death enters the world, 2:19	Death is no more, 21:4
Humanity is cast out of paradise, 3:24	Humanity is restored to paradise, 22:14
Sorrow and pain begin, 3:17	Sorrow, tears, and pain end, 21:4

Regarding knowledge of heaven, we must humbly recognize our limits.

The secret things belong to the Lord our God, but the things revealed belong to us and to our children forever. —Deuteronomy 29:29

- Mystery requires faith to know that God is in control.
- We do not need to know everything.
- We know all that we need to be faithful and obedient.

What happens when people die?

When one experiences the loss of a loved one, the pain of the loss makes it difficult to focus on the ultimate destination. The immediate concern is *what has happened to my loved one? Is my loved one in heaven?*

What will happen to me when I die?

Although some of the details remain hidden, we know that:

- Our life and future are secure in God's hands (Ps. 34:6; 91:4; Is. 25:4; Rom. 8:37–39).

- We go to a place of waiting in the presence of God (1 John 3:2–3). Many theologians call this period between our deaths and Jesus' return the *intermediate state.*

- It is not a permanent place; the whole creation waits for the final redemption at the end of time.

- It is not a place up by the clouds; we do not know where it is, but it is where Jesus is present.

Can we be sure what happens after we die? **Yes!**

- Believers will enjoy the blessing of God's presence (1 John 3:2–3; Rev. 21:22).

- Believers from all of history wait in joy and peace, but with longing, for the return of Christ (Rev. 6:9–10).

- As believers, we will join them at some point.

- When God renews all things, we will all dwell together in the new heavens and the new earth (Rev. 21–22).

Author: Benjamin Galan, MTS, ThM, Adjunct Professor of OT Hebrew and Literature at Fuller Seminary

ROSE BIBLE BASICS:

Myth-Busters

A FREE downloadable version of this study guide is available at rose-publishing.com. Click on "News & Info," then on "Downloads."

The leader guide covers each chapter of this book and includes teaching tips, additional resources, and answer keys for the study guide worksheets. The study guide includes a reproducible worksheet and/or discussion questions for each chapter.

What participants will gain from this study:
- Be encouraged to grow in confidence in their faith.
- Find out why evolution faces a radical challenge from Intelligent Design, and how scientific discoveries point to a Creator.
- Be able to answer common objections to God's existence, biblical reliability, and Jesus' resurrection.
- Learn the difference between true biblical teachings and the destructive ideas of "pop spirituality" teachers, like Eckhart Tolle, Deepak Chopra, and *The Secret*.
- Learn how to answer skeptics' objections to the reliability of the Gospels.
- Know what the Bible teaches—and doesn't teach—about angels, heaven, and the afterlife.

LEADER GUIDE

Spend time in prayer before each study session and pray for each participant.

CHAPTER 1: MYTHS ABOUT GOD & SCIENCE

Main Idea
The natural world displays complex design pointing to a Creator.

Teaching Tips
Introduce participants to the purposes of this study. Ask them what they hope to gain from the study or why they joined the study.

Participants may come to this study with doubts, disagreements, and lots of questions. Create an environment where participants feel safe to ask questions and share their doubts. Do this by maintaining a relaxed, open environment in which questions are welcomed and accepted without negative judgment. Share how you personally have resolved the issue, but allow God to work in other people's minds and hearts in his own way.

This chapter may be confusing for some participants. Do not to expect them to learn everything in one session. Focus on the main concepts you want them to grasp, such as:

- Darwinian evolution is not a proven fact; it cannot explain life's origins or all biological systems.
- Design in the natural world can be detected.
- Design points to an intelligent Creator.

Digging Deeper
Check out the authors' book *Understanding Intelligent Design: Everything You Need to Know in Plain Language* by William Dembski and Sean McDowell (Harvest House: 2008).

Answers to Evolution and *Creation and Evolution* pamphlets, available at www.rose-publishing.com.

For video segments to show, check out the documentary *Where Does the Evidence Lead: Exploring the Theory of Intelligent Design* (Illustra Media: 2004; 60 min.) www.illustramedia.com.

There Is a God: How the World's Most Notorious Atheist Changed His Mind by Antony Flew with Roy Abraham Varghese (Harper One: 2008).

Worksheet Key
(1) f (2) c (3) a (4) b (5) e (6) d (7) g (8) h

CHAPTER 2: MYTHS ABOUT GOD'S EXISTENCE

Main Idea

God exists and has revealed himself through creation, moral conscience, and the Bible.

Teaching Tips

Start the conversation by asking participants to respond to this quote from atheist Sam Harris:

> "There is, in fact, no worldview more reprehensible in its arrogance than that of a religious believer: *the creator of the universe takes an interest in me, approves of me, loves me, and will reward me after death.... Everyone who disagrees with me will spend eternity in hell.* An average Christian, in an average church, listening to an average Sunday sermon has achieved a level of arrogance simply unimaginable in scientific discourse." (*Letter to a Christian Nation* by Sam Harris; paperback ed., Random House: 2006, 2008; p. 74.)

Ask participants: What does this writer find objectionable about Christianity? Do you think most atheists and/or agnostics would agree with this writer's statement?

This chapter contains more material than can be covered in a typical session, so pick only four topics and focus on those. The discussion questions provided correspond to the 10 Q&A in this chapter. Use the discussion questions that relate to the topics you've selected.

Digging Deeper

www.BeThinking.org has short, easy-to-understand articles that can be printed out and made available to participants who want to learn more about a specific topic.

(There is no worksheet provided for this chapter.)

CHAPTER 3: MYTHS ABOUT SPIRITUALITY

Main Idea

The central claims of pop spirituality directly contradict the good news of the gospel.

Teaching Tips

Show the trailer to the movie *The Secret* (www.thesecret.tv). Ask participants: What claims is this promotion making? What do you notice about this promotion and this kind of "spirituality" that is appealing to people?

Have participants practice interpreting the meaning of Scripture in its context.
Read this excerpt from Tolle's book *A New Earth*:

"Blessed are the poor in spirit," Jesus said, "for theirs will be the kingdom of heaven." [Matthew 5:3] What does "poor in spirit" mean? No inner baggage, no identifications. Not with things, nor with any mental concepts that have a sense of self in them. And what is the "kingdom of heaven"? The simple but profound joy of Being that is there when you let go of identification and so become "poor in spirit." (*A New Earth* by Eckhart Tolle; Plume, 2005; p. 43.)

Provide several Bible dictionaries for participants to look up "kingdom of heaven," and Bible commentaries on Matthew 5 to explore what "poor in spirit" meant in Jesus' time. Then ask participants: What are the differences between what Tolle says about these terms and the biblical meaning of these terms? Why is it important to understand what the biblical texts mean in their context?

Digging Deeper
For further study, see the resources listed at the end of the chapter.

Worksheet Key
(1) Myth (2) Myth (3) Truth (4) Myth (5) Myth (6) Myth (7) Truth
(8) Myth

CHAPTER 4: MYTHS ABOUT ANGELS
Main Idea
Angels are God's messengers, but we must remember that God wants us to seek and worship him alone, rather than looking to his angels.

Teaching Tips
Open the session by looking at popular depictions of angels. To show participants different examples, find pictures of angels from the Internet, books, or figurines, etc. (For example: a child-like cherub, warrior angel, angels from Renaissance art, Christmas tree-top angel, abstract angel painting, etc.) Ask participants: What do each of these representations say about what angels are like and what they do? As you teach the lesson, help participants to recognize the difference between these popular ideas of angels and what the Bible says about angels.

Some participants may strongly disagree with this chapter based on their personal experience or the experiences of people they know. Be sensitive to that. Don't put down people's experiences. But *do* use the Bible to help participants understand those experiences in light of Scripture. Stress the importance of examining God's Word to see if those claims or beliefs are the truth (Acts 17:11).

The question *Can a Christian be demon possessed?* may arise during group discussion or teaching time. If it does, explain these things: (1) The difference between demon possession and demon oppression; (2) That believers are indwelt by the Holy Spirit (Rom. 8:9–11, 1 Cor. 3:16, 6:19); and (3) As children of God we have overcome false spirits and do not need to fear them (1 John 4:4).

Digging Deeper
For further study, see the resources listed at the end of the chapter.
Some angel communication practices involve New Age practices and can lead to overt occult activity. See *10 Questions & Answers on Magic, Spells & Divination* pamphlet available at www.rose-publishing.com.

Worksheet Key
(1) humans   (2) angels, God   (3) God   (4) Angels   (5) humans and angels, God   (6) God, angels, humans   (7) God, angels, angels

CHAPTER 5: MYTHS ABOUT JESUS
Main Idea
The New Testament accurately tells us about Jesus' life, ministry, death, and resurrection.

Teaching Tips
There may not be enough time to cover all the topics in this chapter, so encourage participants to pick a few topics that most interest them, and spend the majority of the class time focusing on those topics. Or, if you prefer, choose the topics yourself before the session and focus on those.
To get the conversation started, play a clip of *The Da Vinci Code* movie where references to the *Gospel of Mary Magdalene* are made (approximately 60 minutes into the movie). Ask participants: What claims or assumptions are the characters making about Jesus? About the Gospels? About Christianity?

Digging Deeper
For a video segment to show during this session check out the DVD *The Real Jesus: A Defense of the Historicity & Divinity of Christ* (The Apologetics Group: 2008).
For more on specific topics mentioned in this chapter see *Gospels: "Lost" & Found* which discusses the Gnostic gospels, and *50 Proofs for the New Testament* which explains archeological finds, both available at www.rose-publishing.com.

Worksheet Key
(1) d   (2) False   (3) c   (4) False   (5) a

CHAPTER 6: MYTHS ABOUT THE BIBLE

Main Idea
We can be confident that our Bible today is faithful to the original manuscripts.

Teaching Tips
Some participants may have strong feelings about this topic. If you have a disruptive participant remember these things: (1) Don't get angry; It will only escalate tensions and become personal; (2) Tell the participant that you appreciate his/her input and participation; (3) Don't start a debate between you and the participant; Rather, open up the discussion with the group and ask for other participants' input; (4) See it as a teaching moment; By your example, you can show the group how to have a respectful conversation.

During the session have participants read these key passages: John 21:24–25; Luke 1:1–4; John 20:30–31; 1 Cor. 15:3–7; 2 Peter 1:20–21; 2 Tim. 3:16. Ask participants: What do these passages tell us about how the New Testament writers viewed their own writings? What do these passages tell us about how the writers viewed the Old Testament?

Digging Deeper
To go into more detail about the topics in this chapter, see the author's book, *Misquoting Truth* by Timothy Paul Jones (InterVarsity Press: 2007).

Download the FREE twelve-slide PowerPoint® on the Gnostic *Gospel of Judas* from www.rose-publishing.com (key word: "Gospel of Judas") to illustrate the kind of content in the Gnostic gospels. (If you do not have a computer and projector available, print out the individual slides and give copies to participants.)

Worksheet Key
(1) False   (2) True   (3) c   (4) c   (5) False

CHAPTER 7: MYTHS ABOUT HEAVEN

Main Idea

Heaven is at the heart of God's plan for creation; It's all we ever dreamt and more.

Teaching Tips

The issue of near-death experiences may arise during group discussion or teaching time. If it does, remind participants: (1) It is difficult to know what is happening in the unconscious mind during medical/physical trauma, so we should not be quick to rely on every near-death experience story; (2) Always compare personal testimonies against what Scripture says; and (3) Focus on what we *do* know about heaven that has been revealed in the Bible.

Digging Deeper

"What Will Heaven Be Like?" by Peter Kreeft (6/1/03), available at www. christianitytoday.com/ct/2003/juneweb-only/6-2-51.0.html

Surprised by Hope: Rethinking Heaven, the Resurrection, and the Mission of the Church by N.T. Wright (Harper One: 2008).

Journey into the Light: Exploring Near-Death Experiences by Richard Abanes (Baker: 1996).

Worksheet Key

(1) False   (2) False   (3) e   (4) c   (5) True

FEEDBACK

To improve future studies, be sure to get feedback from the group about teaching style, meeting location, discussion time, material covered, length of study, and group size. Choose a method that best suits your group: Anonymous evaluation sheet, e-mail response or questionnaire, open discussion. (See the feedback questions at the end of the study guide.)

Note: The inclusion of a work or website does not necessarily mean endorsement of all its contents or of other works by the same author(s).

STUDY GUIDE

The study guide which begins on the following page includes a reproducible worksheet and/or discussion questions for group discussion or personal reflection.

MYTHS ABOUT GOD & SCIENCE

Worksheet

Match the key terms with their definitions.

a. Small-scale evolution in which organisms adapt to their environment.

1. _____ Intelligent Design

b. The supposed evolutionary process that produces entirely new species.

c. Something that is hard to reproduce by chance and matches an independently given pattern. This is a scientific method for detecting design.

2. _____ Specified Complexity

3. _____ Microevolution

d. The process by which nature "selects" the fittest organisms to survive. In Darwinian evolution this an unguided material process that gives no evidence of purpose or design.

4. _____ Macroevolution

e. The method in which science is the search for naturalistic explanations of the world. This limits science to purely material explanations.

5. _____ Methodological Naturalism

f. The study of patterns in nature that are best explained as the result of intelligence.

6. _____ Natural Selection

g. This describes a system where if one part is missing the entire system cannot function. Evolution could not develop a system like this.

7. _____ Irreducible Complexity

h. The worldview that sees the universe as a self-contained system of matter and energy that operates by unbroken natural laws, thus everything in the universe is the result of chance and necessity, not the purposeful design by God.

8. _____ Naturalism

Discussion Questions

1. What arguments for ID do you find most convincing?
2. What are some examples of the naturalism worldview in pop culture, education, and the media?
3. Does ID prove the existence of the Christian God as revealed in the Bible? Why or why not?
4. How important is it for Christians to know what they believe about evolution? Can someone be a Christian and believe in evolution?
5. What questions do you still have about this topic and would like to learn more about?

MYTHS ABOUT GOD'S EXISTENCE

Discussion Questions

1. What do the terms *atheism* and *agnosticism* mean?
   In your experience, are most of the people who don't believe in God atheists or agnostics?
   How do you typically react when you hear people deny God's existence?

2. What are some reasons people say they have for not believing in God?
   Do you find the arguments for God's existence convincing?

3. Why is it so difficult to live as a moral relativist? Give some examples (hypothetical or real) where it's clearly not best to claim that *all* moral values are really just made up by humans.

4. Do you think there is a *cultural* conflict in society between science and Christianity, or an *actual* conflict—or both? Why or why not?

5. Often we hear claims in the media that science has discovered the explanation for why we are happy, why we fall in love, why praying helps, and even why we believe in God. What are some reasons people look to science to explain their lives? What do you do when scientific explanations and biblical explanations appear to be different?

6. When we see evil in the world, it's easy to doubt God's goodness. What do you do when you doubt?
   How would you help a friend who is doubting?

7. What are the biggest challenges to seeking justice today?
   Read Luke 4:18. What are some ways you have seen God use people to bring "good news" to the poor and freedom to the oppressed?

8. How important is it to your faith that the Bible accurately record historical events?
   Do you feel confident to defend the reliability of the Bible? Why or why not?

9. How would you explain to a naturalist (someone who believes that only physical things exist) what a soul is?
   According to John 3:16 what is required of someone to have eternal life? Is there anything else people need to do to be saved?

10. Are all meanings and purposes in life equally as good for someone to have?
    How does having a meaning and purpose that aligns with the God's purposes change one's life?

MYTHS ABOUT SPIRITUALITY

Worksheet

Circle "Myth" or "Truth" for each statement.

1. There is no separation between you and God.	Myth	Truth
2. You determine your own purpose in life.	Myth	Truth
3. God is the ultimate standard of right and wrong.	Myth	Truth
4. There are many paths that lead to God which don't require a belief in Jesus Christ.	Myth	Truth
5. Tragedy happens to you because of your imperfect thinking.	Myth	Truth
6. You are the truth just like Jesus is the truth.	Myth	Truth
7. Jesus made it clear that he was God.	Myth	Truth
8. Heaven in the Bible refers to the realm of inner consciousness.	Myth	Truth

Discussion Questions

1. Why are the teachings of pop spirituality dangerous to a believer's walk with God?
2. Why is it important to understand what Bible verses mean in their context?
3. Suppose a friend asked you, "How can pop spirituality teachers be wrong when they bring peace to so many people?" How would you answer this?
4. Read Colossians 1:9. Where does true spiritual wisdom come from?
5. Read 1 Corinthians 2:6–13. What role does the Holy Spirit have in our spirituality?
6. What does "salvation" mean to pop spirituality teachers, and how is this different than what the Bible teaches that salvation means?

MYTHS ABOUT ANGELS

Worksheet

Fill in the blanks with "angels," "humans," or "God."

1. When believers die, they are raised as glorified _____ with bodies like Christ's.

2. Fallen _____ can possess people and cause illnesses, but _____ has complete authority over them.

3. Believers should seek spiritual guidance from _____.

4. _____ are spirits without bodies.

5. Both _____ and _____ should glorify and worship _____ alone.

6. As _____'s messengers, _____ will *not* bring new revelation to _____ that contradicts what has been revealed in the Bible.

7. There is no biblical support for the idea that _____ gives some people a special faith in the ministry of _____ so they are more likely to see _____.

Discussion Questions

1. After reading this chapter, what did you learn about angels that you previously didn't know or misunderstood? What caught your attention the most?

2. Why do you think some people—including Christians—look to angels instead of God for guidance and comfort?

3. How much should we believe about angels based on personal testimony about angel encounters?

4. Many TV shows and movies depict angels differently than the Bible. Is there danger in watching this entertainment? Why or why not?

5. Read 1 Peter 3:22 and Romans 8:37–39. Why don't believers need to fear fallen angels (demons) or other spiritual powers?

MYTHS ABOUT JESUS

Worksheet

1. What are the "Gnostic Gospels"?
    a. Gospels based on the book of Matthew
    b. Writings that portray more accurately who Jesus was
    c. Writings that include eyewitness testimony about Jesus
    d. Writings produced in the second and third centuries AD

2. True or False? The first-century historian Josephus does <u>not</u> mention Jesus in his writings.

3. Which is <u>not</u> true about the Buddhist manuscript Notovitch claimed to discover in the 18th century?
    a. The manuscript was claimed to be discovered in a Buddhist monastery.
    b. Notovitch claimed the manuscript described how Jesus traveled around India.
    c. The manuscript that he claimed was discovered in India was actually discovered in Egypt.
    d. No manuscript has been produced to verify Notovich's claims that it even exists.

4. True or False? All rabbis in Jesus' time were required to be married.

5. Which is true about the "Jesus Family Tomb"?
    a. Joseph and Jesus were common names in the first century.
    b. Most biblical scholars accept the "Jesus family tomb" theory.
    c. It provides proof that Jesus and Mary Magdalene were married.
    d. (a) and (b)

Discussion Questions

1. When you hear challenges to Jesus' existence or the reliability of the Gospels, how do you usually respond?
2. Why do you think that in recent years more and more people are eager to remake Jesus into a New Age practitioner or an Eastern guru?
3. How would you respond to this objection: "Everyone knows that Jesus didn't rise from the dead—Christians just believe that on blind faith."
4. Read 1 Corinthians 15:12–18. Why is Jesus' resurrection important for our salvation?
5. What is one topic in this chapter that you would like to learn more about?

MYTHS ABOUT THE BIBLE

Worksheet

1. True or False? With reckless abandon, the New Testament writers changed the oral tradition about Jesus.

2. True or False? The sources of the Gospels were likely eyewitnesses of events of Jesus' life.

3. The word *canon*:
   a. Comes from a Greek word meaning "a group of books."
   b. Refers to the first four books of the New Testament.
   c. Comes from a Greek word meaning "measuring stick."
   d. Refers to the Trinity in the Gospels.

4. Most of the 400,000 variations in New Testament manuscripts:
   a. Affect doctrinal issues.
   b. Show the significance of the poor quality of copying.
   c. Are minor spelling errors and variations of word order.
   d. Show that the Bible is not reliable.

5. True or False? What matters most is the *age* of the existing manuscripts <u>not</u> their *reliability* when compared.

Discussion Questions

1. Read 2 Timothy 3:14–16. Why is the reliability of "holy Scriptures" important?

2. There have been many attacks on the reliability of the Bible, especially the Gospels. Why do you think this has become so common?

3. Does the fact that we do not have the original manuscripts of the New Testament affect the reliability of the Bible in any way? Why or why not?

4. Does it matter whether the Gospel accounts of Jesus' life are reliable? Why or why not?

5. How has the information from this chapter helped your understanding and trust of the Bible?

MYTHS ABOUT HEAVEN

Worksheet

1. True of False? The physical world is evil, so we must focus on the spiritual which is good.

2. True of False? None of the features of this world will continue in the renewed creation.

3. Which of the following will end in the renewed creation?
   a. Marriage
   b. Death
   c. Work
   d. All of the above
   e. (a) and (b)

4. In heaven we will worship God always; This means that we will all:
   a. Sing hymns day and night.
   b. Be in church every day.
   c. Have an attitude of awe, gratitude, humility, and love.
   d. Be really bored.

5. True or False? Christ is the first example or "firstfruits" of all who will be raised into new life.

Discussion Questions

1. What do you remember learning about heaven when you were growing up?

2. At what times in your life do most reflect on the afterlife? Give an example.

3. In what ways does having a belief in the reality of heaven change the way we live our lives now?

4. How can a person be sure that he or she will go to heaven?

5. What questions do you still have about heaven and would like to learn more about?

FEEDBACK

1. What did you learn through this study that deepened your relationship with God and/or helped you understand biblical teachings better?

_____

_____

2. What was your favorite thing about this study, and why?

_____

_____

3. How could the meeting location, setting, length, or time be improved?

_____

_____

4. Did you think the material covered was too difficult, too easy, or just right?

_____

_____

5. What would you like to see different about the group discussions?

_____

_____

6. What would you like to see different about the activities?

_____

_____

7. What topic would you like to learn more about?

_____

_____

MORE Rose Bible Basics
Bible Reference Made Easy

Where to Find It in the Bible
Handy, full-color companion for Bible study and teaching. Helps you locate:
- Your favorite Bible verses by topic
- 100 prayers in the Bible
- Important people of the Bible
- 100 prophecies fulfilled by Jesus
- 52 key Bible stories

Provides a one-year Bible reading plan, basics of Bible study, and a harmony of the Gospels. Includes study guide.
128 pages, 6 x 9-inch paperback ISBN: 9781596363441

Jesus
This easy-to-understand book provides a biblically centered approach to learning who Jesus is and why his powerful message of salvation matters today. Includes: the Gospels side by side, 50 names of Jesus, the Beatitudes and the Lord's Prayer. Learn how to confront popular myths about Jesus, and to show that he is truly the Messiah (the Christ)—the hope of all people for all time!

Packed with full-color photos, illustrations and charts, as well as numerous Bible verses and references for further study. Perfect for new believers classes, Bible studies, personal study, or as a handy Bible reference. Includes study guide.
128 pages, 6 x 9-inch paperback ISBN: 9781596363243

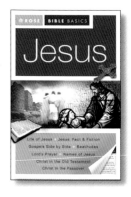

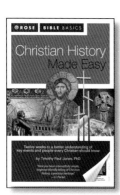

Christian History Made Easy
This easy-to-read book brings to life the most important events and people in Christian history that every believer should know. Author Timothy Paul Jones, Ph.D., makes Christian history refreshingly fun while at the same time informative and engaging. From kings to monks, revivals to revolutions—follow the fascinating history of the Christian faith from the time of Jesus to today.
Easy to use in the classroom, at church, for homeschooling or personal study. Includes study guide.
224 pages, 6 x 9-inch paperback ISBN: 9781596363281

God in Real Life
To navigate life's tough choices, teens and young adults need a real relationship with God in their real life. This full-color book provides clear, biblical answers to their questions about Jesus, Christianity, other religions, pop occultism, evolution, sex, decision making, faith, and growing closer to God.

Great for youth groups, Bible studies, new believers, or anyone who wants to understand what it means to be a follower of Jesus at school, at home, and with friends. Includes study guide.
128 pages, 6 x 9-inch paperback ISBN: 9781596363250